Scott Aniol

importance. His commitment to the authority of Scripture as revealed truth; the centrality of the gospel as the intended message of Scripture; the prerogative, initiative, and glory of God as the telos of Scripture; and specific directions for corporate worship as a consistent theme of Scripture permeates his discussions of gospel-shaped worship. Every person responsible for shaping and leading corporate worship should read this book with a serious intent of allowing its arguments and its presentation of examples be considered seriously as a matter of conscience. Christian congregations will find their times together as God-centered, Word-centered, gospel-centered persuasives to conviction, confession, assurance, holiness, and witness.

– **Tom J. Nettles**
Professor Emeritus,
The Southern Baptist Theological Seminary

Scott Aniol has provided an excellent book for understanding the importance of recognizing the Word of God as the authority of corporate worship and the practical implications that flow from grounding our theology of worship in the Scriptures. The book's clarity and conciseness make it particularly accessible by the layperson who wants to learn foundational principles of worship and helpful for the church leader or pastor who wants to refine his articulation of biblical worship. I look forward to getting this in the hands of the worshipers God has tasked me with shepherding.

– **Laramie Minga**
Pastor, Worship and Discipleship
Woodlawn Baptist Church, Baton Rouge, LA

The devilish attack of deformation transcends beyond the doctrines of Scripture to the functionality of the church. The church and Scripture are inextricably bound together. Therefore, the need of the hour is biblical reformation of the church's worship. Scott Aniol does an excellent job of directing our attention to Scripture and warning us of the steady stream of man-centered worship philosophies constantly luring Christians outside the boundaries of Scripture.

– Josh Buice
Pastor, Pray's Mill Baptist Church, Douglasville, GA
President, G3 Ministries

Biblical Foundations for Corporate Worship is no empty title. For a subject that can be so easily hijacked by personal preferences, cultural fads, or denominational snobbery, in these pages you will hear the authoritative voice of Scripture alone speaking. I am grateful that Aniol, already a trusted scholar in the field, has delved again into the world of worship to produce this useful resource. If you want help exploring all the Bible says about the praise of God's people, start here.

– Jonathan Landry Cruse, Pastor, Author,
Hymns of Devotion **and** *What Happens When We Worship*

Semper Reformanda—"always reforming"—is the church's call. With the embrace of Reformed theology, many begin with soteriology and the doctrines of grace. Few think of what it means to regulate worship based solely on the instruction of Scripture. In *Biblical Foundations of Corporate Worship*, Scott Aniol starts by challenging this audience to examine worship through the lens of God's revelation in Scripture.

As Scripture shapes our thinking, it should also shape our worship of God. This book is a fantastic foundation for many in the church who have embraced Reformed doctrine in expositional preaching but have yet to apply these biblical truths to every facet of corporate worship. Scott reminds us in the book that well-intentioned ideas about worship that do not begin with God's revelation of himself are, at best, short-sighted and, at worst, reflective of a low view of God. This book is a must-read for those who have not applied these ideas to corporate worship and an excellent Bible-saturated reminder for those who have made proper applications.

– Virgil Walker
Executive Director of Operations, G3 Ministries

Biblical Foundations
of
Corporate Worship

Scott Aniol

Biblical Foundations *of* Corporate Worship

Scott Aniol

Biblical Foundations of Corporate Worship
Copyright © 2022 by Scott Aniol

All rights reserved. No part of this book may be used or reproduced in any manner whatsoever without written permission except in the case of brief quotations embodied in critical articles and reviews. Direct your requests to the publisher at the following address:

Published by

Free Grace Press
3900 Dave Ward Dr., Ste. 1900
Conway, AR 72034
(501) 214-9663
email: support@freegracepress.com
website: www.freegracepress.com

Cover design by Joe Zarate

Printed in the United States of America

Scripture quotations are from the ESV® Bible (The Holy Bible, English Standard Version®), copyright © 2001 by Crossway, a publishing ministry of Good News Publishers. Used by permission. All rights reserved.

ISBN: 978-1-952599-47-7

For additional Reformed Baptist titles, please email us for a free list or see our website at the above address.

Contents

Corporate Worship's Authority:
The Word of God   1

Corporate Worship's Goal:
Communion with God   27

Corporate Worship's Structure:
Dialogue with God   47

Corporate Worship's Participants:
The Whole Congregation   67

Corporate Worship's Essence:
Spiritual Response   85

Example Covenant Renewal Service Orders   105

1

Corporate Worship's Authority: The Word of God

Ever since Cain and Abel, God's people have been asking, "What is the proper way to worship God?" Uncertainty reigns today in churches over whether certain service elements are truly helpful for congregational worship. What is acceptable? Some godly Christians, attempting to enhance their worship, believe they have freedom to use anything in their worship they think is good. Other godly Christians may then be constrained to participate in something that goes against their consciences. So, how can we be certain the elements we are including in our worship are indeed pleasing to God?

Jesus Christ confronted this issue head on in his day, since the Pharisees had added traditions to the religious life of the Jews that went beyond what God himself had commanded. We find one such confrontation in Mark 7, and it will help to introduce us to the critical importance of biblical authority over our worship.

> Now when the Pharisees gathered to him, with some of the scribes who had come from Jerusalem, they saw that some of his disciples ate with hands that were defiled, that is, unwashed. (For the Pharisees and all the Jews do not eat unless they wash their hands properly, holding to the tradition of the elders, and when they come from the marketplace, they do not eat unless they wash. And there are many other traditions that they observe, such as the washing of cups and pots and copper vessels and dining couches.) And the Pharisees and the scribes asked him, "Why do your disciples not walk according to the tradition of the elders, but eat with defiled hands?" (Mark 7:1–5).

THE TRADITIONS OF MEN

It's important to recognize that the Pharisees' concern here was not over hygiene but rather, worship. They were concerned with ceremonial cleansing that they taught was necessary to worship God correctly. And so, Jesus addresses their concern:

> And he said to them, "Well did Isaiah prophesy of you hypocrites, as it is written,
>
> "'This people honors me with their lips,
>
> > but their heart is far from me;
>
> in vain do they worship me,
>
> > teaching as doctrines the commandments of men.'
>
> You leave the commandment of God and hold to the tradition of men."
>
> And he said to them, "You have a fine way of rejecting the commandment of God in order to establish your tradition!" (Mark 7:6–9)

Jesus condemned the Pharisees for their hypocritical worship; he actually says their worship is vain. But notice why he argues their worship is worthless: they are teaching as doctrines the commandments of men. The Pharisees had gone *beyond* what God had commanded in their worship and added other requirements. And Jesus says, because of this, they have essentially rejected the commandment of God.

Jesus continues by listing some of the other religious requirements the Pharisees have added beyond what God had commanded. But notice what he says later in verse 13: "thus making void the word of God by your tradition that you have handed down. And many such things you do." Jesus is again saying that by adding man-made requirements to worship, the Pharisees are not trusting in the authority and sufficiency of Scripture for their worship, and thus, their worship is vain.

This confrontation between Jesus and the Pharisees provides a core principle that must govern any discussion of worship. Amid so much controversy over worship today, we must remain firmly convinced of this: the bedrock truth on which all our theology and practice of corporate worship must be founded is the authority and sufficiency of Scripture.

The Authority and Sufficiency of Scripture

The key biblical text that emphasizes the authority of God's Word is 2 Timothy 3:16–17:

> All Scripture is breathed out by God and profitable for teaching, for reproof, for correction, and for training in righteousness, that the man of God may be complete, equipped for every good work.

Scripture was literally breathed out by the Spirit of God, and thus the Bible contains all the authority of God within its pages. This inspired revelation is authoritative and sufficient to teach us, to reprove us, to correct us, and to train us in righteousness. The Word of God is authoritative and sufficient to perfectly equip us for every good work, including—or perhaps better, *especially*—the good work for which we were created, the worship of God. Therefore, all our theology and practice of corporate worship must be founded in the authority and sufficiency of what God has spoken—his divine revelation.

This is exactly why seventeenth-century Puritans and Baptists objected to the Church of England, which had added worship rituals and requirements beyond what the New Testament teaches. They insisted on what would later be called *the regulative principles of worship*. The 1644 London Baptist Confession says it this way:

> The rule of this knowledge, faith, and obedience, concerning the worship and service of God, and all other Christian duties, is not man's inventions, opinions, devices, laws, constitutions, or traditions unwritten whatsoever, but only the Word of God contained in the Canonical Scriptures.

The Authority of Scripture over Worship

The authority and sufficiency of Scripture is a critical doctrine to grasp for every aspect of our lives as Christians, but it is vital when we think about worship, and there are three primary biblical reasons.

Worship Depends on God's Revelation

First, the very idea of worship begins with God's self-revelation. Worship exists only because God revealed himself. God's speaking the world into existence was in its very essence an act to create worship. God created the universe out of nothing through his spoken word for the express purpose of displaying his own glory (Ps. 19:1), and he created Adam in his image so Adam might witness that glory and respond in worship. God's chief end is to glorify himself, and he calls all men everywhere to fulfill their purpose in life by doing the same (Isa. 43:6–7).

Yet this desire to be worshiped did not stop with speaking the world into existence. Creation certainly displays the glory of God, but creation alone is not enough to reveal the God to be worshiped. Adam would not have known whom he was supposed to worship except that God spoke to him. God revealed himself to Adam and told him of his purpose in Genesis 2:15: "The Lord God took the man and put him in the garden of Eden to work it and keep it." The phrase "work it and keep it" seems to imply that Adam's purpose was to garden, yet the work of gardening would not have been necessary prior to the fall. Rather, the two verbs in this phrase have a deeper significance. Most of the time when they are used together in the Old Testament, they refer to the priestly duties of the Levites in the tabernacle. Thus, from within a pre-fall context and with an understanding of the meaning and use of these verbs, what Genesis 2:15 reveals is God's declaration that man's purpose is to worship and obey. God spoke his revelation to Adam so that he might worship.

The fact that God's first words created the very existence of worship leads to a recognition that all worship begins with what God said. God is the initiator of worship, and in particular, God's revelation of himself is what provides the basis for all true worship. Our corporate worship must be grounded in the authoritative, sufficient Word of God.

God Rejects Worship He Has Not Prescribed

Second, throughout Scripture, examples abound of God rejecting worship that includes elements he has not prescribed. Rarely are these elements introduced with malicious intent—usually the motive is to enhance the worship of Yahweh. But God nevertheless rejects worship that includes such extra-biblical elements. One of the most striking examples is found in Leviticus 10:

> Now Nadab and Abihu, the sons of Aaron, each took his censer and put fire in it and laid incense on it and offered unauthorized fire before the Lord, which he had not commanded them. And fire came out from before the Lord and consumed them, and they died before the Lord. Then Moses said to Aaron, "This is what the Lord has said: 'Among those who are near me I will be sanctified, and before all the people I will be glorified.'" And Aaron held his peace. (Lev. 10:1–3)

In this passage Nadab and Abihu offered an unauthorized fire to the Lord and were killed for it. Why were they killed? Nothing was inherently evil or profane about what they were doing. But they were killed because, as verse 1 says, the Lord had not commanded this element of worship. God is very serious about this. The only acceptable worship is that which he himself has commanded.

We have already seen this same problem with the Pharisees of the New Testament, but it continued later in the early church with the "Judaizers," Christian converts who taught it was necessary to adopt Jewish religious practices from the law of Moses. The church first encountered this when some Jewish Christian converts traveled to Antioch and insisted to the Christians there, "Unless you are circumcised according to the custom of Moses, you cannot be saved" (Acts 15:1). This resulted in the formation of a council of church leadership in Jerusalem, including James, Peter, and Paul, to debate the matter. The council concluded that requiring such religious practices not prescribed for the church was "a yoke on the neck of the disciples" (v. 10).

Again, the bottom line is that God alone has the right to determine how we worship, and he has communicated sufficient revelation for how he desires to be worshiped in his inspired Word. Therefore, we must be sure that how we are worshiping is what God has prescribed. The Second London Baptist Confession (2LBC) puts it this way:

> But the acceptable way of worshipping the true God, is instituted by himself, and so limited by his own revealed will, that he may not be worshipped according to the imagination and devices of men, nor the suggestions of Satan, under any visible representations, or any other way not prescribed in the Holy Scriptures. (22.1)

God's Authority Limits the Church's Authority

Third, Scripture is clear that Christians have liberty of conscience in spiritual matters. In other words, no Christian may be expected to participate in a spiritual practice he is not "convinced in his own mind" is necessary (Rom. 14:5). This limits even pastoral authority. No pastor or other church leader has the authority to impose on another believer a spiritual practice that does not have explicit biblical warrant—no matter how much it may have "an appearance of wisdom" (Col. 2:20–23).

This principle is clearly laid out in the New Testament because in the early years of the church, some Christians insisted on introducing Jewish worship elements into Christian worship—elements that had not been prescribed for church worship. Paul deals with this issue specifically in Romans 14:5–6:

> One person esteems one day as better than another, while another esteems all days alike. Each one should be fully convinced in his own mind. The one who observes the day, observes it in honor of the Lord. The one who eats, eats in honor of the Lord, since he gives thanks to God, while the one who abstains, abstains in honor of the Lord and gives thanks to God.

In Romans 14, Paul is dealing specifically with those Christian Jews who desire to maintain religious restrictions and observances from the Mosaic law. The key thing to remember here is that these are religious restrictions of ceremonially unclean food and observances of sacred days. Any proper discussion of so-called Christian liberty must be framed in this context. In other words, while 1 Corinthians 8–10 applies to general things with negative associations from the pagan world, like meat offered to idols, Romans 14 deals with the more narrowed topic of adding requirements to religious life. So, this passage has direct application to the issue of public worship, and the formulators of the regulative principles applied it that way.

With the intent to "pursue what makes for peace and mutual upbuilding" (v. 19), Paul insists in verse 5 that "each one should be fully convinced in his own mind" concerning sacred days, and in verse 23, he warns that "whoever has doubts is condemned if he eats, because the eating is not from faith. For whatever does not proceed from faith is sin." The question is, should we observe sacred days that have not been prescribed for church worship? Paul says that to institute something like that, each person must be convinced in his own mind. One must be careful not to impose on his own conscience or the conscience of another that of which they are not fully convinced.

And what is the only way we can be convinced that God wants us to observe a particular sacred day? Only if he has prescribed it for the church. If you as an individual are convinced for some reason that you should observe it, then you have every right to do so in your home. But we cannot extend such observance to gatherings of the church where we have many individual consciences that must be convinced from the Word of God that such an observance is necessary.

This issue is also addressed in Colossians 2:20–23:

> If with Christ you died to the elemental spirits of the world, why, as if you were still alive in the world, do you submit to regulations—"Do not handle, Do not taste, Do not touch" (referring to things that all perish as they are used)—according to human precepts and teachings? These have indeed an appearance of wisdom in promoting self-made religion and asceticism and severity to the body, but they are of no value in stopping the indulgence of the flesh.

Here Paul is chiding Christians who are adding to their religious life elements that are merely requirements of men. Again, these "Do not handle, Do not taste, Do not touch" requirements are in the context of the body (vv.

18–19) and are referencing specific religious restrictions carried over from the Mosaic law. Paul is saying that for the sake of the unity of the body, we must limit ourselves to religious requirements clearly prescribed in the New Testament. He even says that these kinds of things do indeed have an appearance of wisdom and spirituality. But because they have not been commanded by God, they render the worship unacceptable to him.

Again, in the seventeenth century, Puritans (later, Presbyterians) and Baptists insisted on biblical authority over worship practice, not to unnecessarily restrict corporate worship but to liberate stricken consciences from practices within corporate worship not expressly set forth in the Scriptures. They insisted that no man, including someone in authority, had the right to constrain a worshiper to participate in an activity of worship that had no Scriptural directive. The Second London Baptist Confession summarizes the point well:

> God alone is Lord of the conscience, and hath left it free from the doctrines and commandments of men which are in any thing contrary to his word, or not contained in it. So that to believe such doctrines, or obey such commands out of conscience, is to betray true liberty of conscience; and the requiring of an implicit

faith, an absolute and blind obedience, is to destroy liberty of conscience and reason also. (2LBC 21.2)

This principle, far from being restrictive, is actually quite liberating. Pastors do not need to worry about chasing after the latest popular worship fads or conducting preference polls of their people. Likewise, church members need not fear the next worship novelty, nor will they need to deliberate over what best worship practices they should adopt. The church simply follows the clear instructions of Scripture.

John Fawcett, an English Baptist pastor in the mid-1700s, summarized this characteristically Baptist conviction:

> No acts of worship can properly be called holy, but such as the Almighty has enjoined. No man, nor any body of men have any authority to invent rites and ceremonies of worship; to change the ordinances which he has established; or to invent new ones . . . The divine word is the only safe directory in what relates to his own immediate service. The question is not what we may think becoming, decent or proper, but what our gracious Master has authorized as such. In matters of religion, noth-

ing bears the stamp of holiness but what God has ordained.[1]

The Extent of Biblical Authority over Worship

So what would it mean, then, for our worship to be truly governed by the authority and sufficiency of Scripture? This emphasis on biblical authority over our corporate worship applies in at least four areas.

Elements

First, the elements of our worship must be regulated by the Word of God. The sufficient Word has given those ordinary means of grace that, through their regular use, will shape believers to live as disciples who observe everything Jesus taught.

Paul commands Timothy, in the context of teaching him how to behave in the house of God, to devote himself to "the *public reading of Scripture*" (1 Tim. 4:13). He repeats similar commands in Colossians 4:16 and 1 Thessalonians 5:27.

He also commands Timothy to devote himself "to exhortation, to teaching" (1 Tim. 4:13) and to "*preach*

---
[1] John Fawcett, *The Holiness Which Becometh the House of the Lord* (Halifax: Holden and Dawson, 1808), 25.

the word; be ready in season and out of season; reprove, rebuke, and exhort, with complete patience and teaching" (2 Tim. 4:2).

Third, Paul commands that "supplications, prayers, *intercessions*, and thanksgivings be made for all people, for kings and all who are in high positions" (1 Tim. 2:1–2). He commands the Colossians to "continue steadfastly in prayer" (4:2), and to the Ephesians he urges them to pray "at all times in the Spirit, with all prayer and supplication . . . making supplication for all the saints" (6:18).

A fourth biblically prescribed element might not be a separate element at all but may be another form of Scripture reading or prayer, and that is *singing*. In two of Paul's letters, he commands gathered believers to sing psalms, hymns, and spiritual songs, thereby "singing and making melody to the Lord with your heart" (Eph. 5:19) and "teaching and admonishing one another in all wisdom" (Col. 3:16).

Fifth, Paul instructs the Corinthian church, "on the first day of every week, each of you is to put something aside and store it up, as he may prosper, so that there will be no collecting when I come" (1 Cor. 16:2). Although in its immediate context this refers to giving that would be taken to needy believers in Jerusalem (v. 3), Paul indicates that elders should be paid (1 Tim. 5:17–18). So, it is fitting that such regular, weekly *giving* be used for that purpose as well, in addition to caring for the particular needs of members in the congregation (Acts 6:1; 1 Tim. 5:3) and other material functions of the church.

Sixth, Christ commands in his Great Commission to the disciples, "Go therefore and make disciples of all nations, *baptizing* them in the name of the Father and of the Son and of the Holy Spirit" (Matt. 28:19).

And finally, Paul tells the Corinthian church that he delivered "*the Lord's supper*" to the church, having received it from the Lord himself (1 Cor. 11:20, 23).

These are the only corporate worship elements given to the church in the New Testament for the purpose of building up the body into mature disciple/worshipers. To add or subtract from these God-ordained elements would be to distrust the sufficiency of God's Word in giving us what we need to equip us for every good work (2 Tim. 3:17). So, the first way our worship is regulated by Scripture is in the elements we choose to include.

Content

Second, the content of our worship elements must be regulated by the Word of God. Paul says to preach *the Word* (2 Tim. 4:2) He says that when we sing, we must "let *the Word* of Christ dwell richly within us" (Col. 3:16) Even our prayers to God should be saturated with Scripture. Put simply, in corporate worship we read the Word, sing the Word, preach the Word, pray the Word, and act out the Word. Our worship is born of, built on, fueled by, governed by, filled with, and sanctified by the truth of God's Word.

Forms

Third, the forms of our worship should be regulated by the Word of God. We must remember that the Bible is not simply a static collection of theological propositions. Rather, Scripture is a collection of God-inspired literary forms that express his truth, and all Scripture, including its aesthetic aspects, carries the weight of divine authority. Therefore, as we choose artistic forms of expression in our modern cultural context, we must be sure that the ways in which those forms communicate truth correspond to the way in which Scripture itself aesthetically communicates truth.

Order

Fourth, the order of our worship should be regulated by the Word of God. If the Bible is our supreme authority, then even the structure of our services should follow what

God has given to us in Scripture. God made clear this purpose when he instituted corporate worship assemblies in the Old Testament, establishing a structural pattern that continues into the New Testament. God often calls these assemblies of worship "memorials." This term meant more than just a passive remembrance of something, but actually a reenactment of God's works in history for his people such that the worshipers are shaped over and over again by what God has done.

Beginning at Mount Sinai (Exodus 19–24), God instituted a particular order of what the Old Testament frequently calls the "solemn assemblies" of Israel. This order reflects what I like to call a "theo-logic," in which God's people reenact, through the order of what they do in the assembly, God's atoning work on their behalf. Here is a summary of this structure:

- God reveals himself and calls his people to worship
- God's people acknowledge and confess their need for forgiveness
- God provides atonement
- God speaks his Word
- God's people respond with commitment
- God hosts a celebratory feast

This same theo-logic characterized the progression of sacrifices within the tabernacle assemblies, moving from the sin offering to the guilt offering to the burnt offering to the grain offering and, finally, to the peace offering. The same structure appears at the dedication of Solomon's temple (2 Chronicles 5–7). In each case, the structure of the worship assemblies follows a theo-logical order in which the worshipers reenact the covenant relationship they have with God through the atonement he provided, culminating with a feast that celebrates the fellowship they enjoy with God because of what he has done for them.

While the particular acts present in Hebrew worship pass away for the New Testament church, the book of Hebrews tells us that these Old Testament rituals were "a copy and shadow of the heavenly things" (8:5). Thus, while the shadows fade away, the theo-logic of corporate worship remains the same: we are reenacting God's atoning work on our behalf when we gather for corporate worship. Significantly, the book of Hebrews teaches that when we gather for services of worship, through Christ we are joining with the real worship taking place in the heavenly Jerusalem. And so, it is important to recognize that the two records we have in Scripture of heavenly worship also follow the same theo-logic modeled in the Old Testament, namely, in Isaiah 6:1–13:

1. God reveals himself and calls his people to worship.

   In the year that King Uzziah died I saw the Lord sitting upon a throne, high and lifted up; and the train of his robe filled the temple. (v. 1)

2. God's people recognize the greatness of God and praise him for it.

   Above him stood the seraphim. Each had six wings: with two he covered his face, and with two he covered his feet, and with two he flew. And one called to another and said: "Holy, holy, holy is the Lord of hosts; the whole earth is full of his glory!" And the foundations of the thresholds shook at the voice of him who called, and the house was filled with smoke. (vv. 2–4)

3. When God's people acknowledge God's holiness, they also recognize their unworthiness to draw near to him because of their sin.

   And I said: "Woe is me! For I am lost; for I am a man of unclean lips, and I dwell in the midst of a people of unclean lips; for my eyes have seen the King, the Lord of hosts!" (v. 5)

4. God's people are assured of pardon through the sacrifice of Christ, which makes worship possible.

> Then one of the seraphim flew to me, having in his hand a burning coal that he had taken with tongs from the altar. And he touched my mouth and said: "Behold, this has touched your lips; your guilt is taken away, and your sin atoned for." (vv. 6–7)

5. The Word of God is taught, and God's people respond to the Word of God with consecration.

> And I heard the voice of the Lord saying, "Whom shall I send, and who will go for us?" Then I said, "Here I am! Send me." And he said, "Go, and say to this people: "'Keep on hearing, but do not understand; keep on seeing, but do not perceive.' Make the heart of this people dull, and their ears heavy, and blind their eyes; lest they see with their eyes, and hear with their ears, and understand with their hearts, and turn and be healed." (vv. 8–10)

6. God's people bring their requests before the Lord.

> Then I said, "How long, O Lord?" (v. 11b)

7. God sends his people into the world to serve him.

Just as the service began with God's Word, it ends with a word of blessing from him.

> And he said: "Until cities lie waste without inhabitant, and houses without people, and the land is a desolate waste, and the Lord removes people far away, and the forsaken places are many in the midst of the land. And though a tenth remain in it, it will be burned again, like a terebinth or an oak, whose stump remains when it is felled." The holy seed is its stump. (vv. 11b–13)

Likewise, when John is given a similar vision of heavenly worship, the order of what happens is the same. From creation to consummation, the corporate worship of God's people is a memorial, a reenactment, of the theo-logic of true worship: God's call for his people to commune with him through the sacrifice of atonement that he has provided, listening to his Word, responding with praise and obedience, and culminating with a beautiful picture of perfect communion with God in the form of a feast. This reenactment in a corporate worship service of God's work for us is what will progressively edify us over time to live out our relationship with God through Christ as his mature disciples and worshipers.

For this reason, historic worship services, intentionally structured on the basis of this biblical theo-logic, have always followed a standard order.

The service opens with God speaking to us. We do not come to worship of our own initiative, and we are not somehow "calling God down" or inviting him to join us. Rather, it is God who calls us to draw near to him, and thus the service begins with a scriptural call to worship.

When God reveals himself to us, two responses are inevitable. First, we respond with adoration and praise. This usually takes the form of a hymn, a prayer of praise, and a doxology. Then we recognize our sin and unworthiness, and so we confess our sins to God. We responded this way when we first believed, and we should continue to do so daily. Thus, through a Scripture reading, a hymn, silent repentance, and a corporate prayer of confession, as a congregation we acknowledge our sin together before God.

As Christians, we find forgiveness and pardon in Christ, and so the service continues with celebrating that forgiveness. Through a Scripture affirmation and a hymn of praise for Christ's sacrifice, we both rejoice in the gospel and proclaim it to any unbelievers who may be attending.

Next, we are ready to hear God's instructions through

the preaching of his Word. Our response is the dedication and giving of our offerings.

The climax of the service is communion with God. Since worship is drawing near to God in communion through Christ, this is what the whole service has been progressing toward. Coming boldly to the throne of grace (Heb. 4:16) for supplication and eating at Christ's Table means that we are welcome and have open access to him, despite our sin. This is possible only through Christ's sacrifice on the cross, which is beautifully pictured in the Communion elements. Communion with God is the purpose of the gospel, and thus Communion is the climax of a worship service.

The service concludes with a word from God in which he sends us into the world to obey him and share the gospel with unbelievers, along with a word of blessing to the congregation.

The hymns, Scripture passages, and other elements of the service are determined by their fit in three categories:

1. We consider the church year, which follows the life of Christ through remembering his coming, ministry, death, resurrection, and ascension.

2. We consider the function of the hymns or Scrip-

ture passages within the Scripture-shaped service order, and that also facilitates the dialogue between God and us in the service.

3. We consider the Scripture passage and theme for the day.

By ordering our corporate worship in this manner, through the course of the church's life, we are submitting the entirety of our corporate worship to the Word of God. If we fail to do this, like the Pharisees, our worship will be vain. But if our worship is inspired, shaped, and guided by who God is, what God does, and what God says—if the primary content and form of our worship services are derived from the Scriptures—we can be sure that our worship will be acceptable to God.

2

Corporate Worship's Goal: Communion with God

In the previous chapter, we established the importance of grounding our theology and practice of worship in the sufficient and authoritative Word of God. The remainder of this book will address the natural question that follows: What theology and practice of worship does the Bible prescribe? And in this chapter, I will consider our goal in corporate worship.

For some today, the main purpose for which they gather is evangelism—every service is designed to bring in seekers and move them toward conversion. For others, the purpose of their gatherings is revival or fellowship. Some see the goal of their gatherings as expressing praise to the

Lord, a few want an emotional experience, and for still others, the gathering is simply a duty to perform. So, what does the Word of God identify as the central goal of our corporate gatherings as a church?

A passage of Scripture that beautifully pictures God's intent for his church is Ephesians 2:11–22.

> Therefore remember that at one time you Gentiles in the flesh, called "the uncircumcision" by what is called the circumcision, which is made in the flesh by hands—remember that you were at that time separated from Christ, alienated from the commonwealth of Israel and strangers to the covenants of promise, having no hope and without God in the world. But now in Christ Jesus you who once were far off have been brought near by the blood of Christ. For he himself is our peace, who has made us both one and has broken down in his flesh the dividing wall of hostility by abolishing the law of commandments expressed in ordinances, that he might create in himself one new man in place of the two, so making peace, and might reconcile us both to God in one body through the cross, thereby killing the hostility. And he came and preached peace to you who were far off and peace to those who were near. For through him

we both have access in one Spirit to the Father. So then you are no longer strangers and aliens, but you are fellow citizens with the saints and members of the household of God, built on the foundation of the apostles and prophets, Christ Jesus himself being the cornerstone, in whom the whole structure, being joined together, grows into a holy temple in the Lord. In him you also are being built together into a dwelling place for God by the Spirit.

The Church: God's Temple

In this portion of Paul's letter to the Ephesians, he is describing the nature of the gospel, which we will discuss more in a moment, but notice the goal of the gospel at the end of this passage. Paul says that as people come to faith in Jesus Christ, they are brought near to him and built into a temple, a dwelling place for God.

This temple metaphor is not coincidental; the gathered New Testament church is the dwelling place for the Spirit of God in this age in the same way that Israel's temple was God's dwelling place in the Old Testament economy. The Bible also teaches that each individual believer is "a temple of the Holy Spirit" (1 Cor. 6:19), but in this passage the focus is on the collective church. Notice verse

21: "in whom the whole structure, being joined together, grows into a holy temple in the Lord."

This way of describing the nature of the church is not unique to Ephesians 2. Paul says in 1 Corinthians 3:16, "Do you not know that you are God's temple and that God's Spirit dwells in you?" Again, it is important to recognize that in this verse the pronouns are plural—you *all* are God's temple—and this is in the context of discussing the church. Paul says the same thing in 2 Corinthians 6:16—*we*, the church, "are the temple of the living God." And Peter says in 1 Peter 2:5 that *Christians* "are being built up as a spiritual house, to be a holy priesthood, to offer spiritual sacrifices acceptable to God through Jesus Christ."

Now why would the New Testament use this image of a temple to describe the gathered church? Well, what most naturally comes to mind when someone uses the image of a temple? You see, Paul is deliberately using this metaphor to signify our central purpose as the gathered church. In this temple, built by the Spirit of God and indwelt by him, worship takes place. So that narrows the answer to our initial question—our goal as a gathered church, the temple of God, is to worship him.

But we still need to explore further to discern what the nature of this worship should be. We might recognize that our purpose when we gather is to worship, but what exactly is that? Is worship merely a duty to perform? Is worship simply expressing hearts of praise to God? Is worship an emotional experience?

If Paul is deliberately using the image of a temple to describe the gathered church, let's take a moment to look at what, exactly, the Old Testament temple (and earlier, the tabernacle) was.

Sanctuary

First, God calls the tabernacle and temple in the Old Testament his *sanctuary*. He told Moses in Exodus 25:8, "Let them make me a sanctuary, that I may dwell in their midst." Calling it a sanctuary communicated the idea of something consecrated and set apart to protect the holiness of God from the uncleanness of everyday life. No uncircumcised or uncleansed person could enter the sanctuary. God gave very clear and specific instructions for how his sanctuary was to be built, how it was to be cared for, and what was required for someone to enter in. The sanctuary and all the elements therein had to be regularly cleansed by the priests. Sinful worshipers had to offer sacrifices of atonement to enter God's sanctuary. And God specifically commanded in Leviticus 19:30, "You shall . . . reverence my sanctuary: I am the Lord."

This idea of set-apartness is then extended to the church as God's temple, which is why Paul calls the church in Ephesians 2:21 "a *holy* temple in the Lord." Paul says in 1 Timothy 3:15 that there is a particular way "to behave" in the church because it is set apart from other gatherings; in fact, he indicates that the entire purpose of writing to Timothy is so that "you may know how one ought to behave" in the gathered church. Something about the assembled church requires behavior that is set apart from conduct in the rest of life. So, while an individual Christian is the temple of God's Spirit and ought to behave in ways that are pleasing to him, the church gathered is, in a special and distinct way, the sanctuary of God's presence, wherein God's people behave in worship differently than in any other circumstances.

As we saw in the last chapter, behavior in the church must be regulated by God's clear instructions in a more explicit manner than for behavior outside the church. Yes, as an individual temple of the Holy Spirit, you may worship God at any time and in any place, whether you eat or drink or whatever you do, but there is a special, set-apart, necessary worship that takes place when we gather as the church. It's not about a building or a particular place, it is about a gathered *people*, the church, the holy temple of God.

House of God

This description of the temple signifies the weight and significance of what we do when we gather to worship, but we must also recognize another important description of the temple in the Old Testament. Several passages in the Old Testament call the tabernacle the "house of God." The same term is used to describe the temple. Second Chronicles 3:3 says Solomon built "the house of God," as do many other Old Testament passages (Ps. 52:8; Ezra 4:24; Neh. 13:11). Again, the question to ask here is what does this image of a house signify about the temple and about the worship that takes place there? As God's house, the temple is where God dwells with his people. Jacob called the place where he met with God "Bethel," which literally means "house of God" (Gen. 28:10–22). A house is where you meet with someone, you dwell with them, you fellowship with them. In other words, this emphasizes the fact that Israel's temple was not simply a place where they performed rituals or had some sort of experience; the temple was where they met with God.

Not surprisingly, the New Testament also refers to the church as God's house. In 1 Timothy 3:15, Paul calls the church "the household of God," and he says in Galatians 6:10 that Christians are "of the household of faith."

Hebrews 10:21 also calls the church "the house of God" and stresses in verse 25 that we must not neglect to meet together. Jesus told his disciples in Matthew 18:20, in the context of talking about the nature of the church, that when the church gathers, Christ is "among them." And we find that very language in Ephesians 2 as well; just before Paul calls the church God's holy temple, he says in verse 19 that believers are "members of the household of God," and in verse 22 he describes the church as "a dwelling place for God."

So, from these two images, *sanctuary* and *house of God*, we can recognize a bit more clearly the nature of who we are and what we are to do as the gathered church—we are a holy, set-apart dwelling place for God, and when we gather, we do not simply perform duties, express praise, or have an experience. When we gather as the church, we meet with God.

Brought Near by the Blood of Christ

However, when we consider these two images together, a problem emerges: If the church is God's temple, God's dwelling place, God's holy sanctuary, how can sinners enter? This is the exact problem Paul in Ephesians 2 is addressing. Beginning in verse 11, he specifically connects the condition of unbelievers with the uncircumcised who were unable to enter Israel's sanctuary. He contrasts through these verses those who are "near"—a term used to indicate those who are able to enter the sanctuary—with those who are "far off"—referring to those prohibited from entering. "But now," he says in verse 13, "in Christ Jesus you who once were far off have been brought near by the blood of Christ." This is language that describes the gospel, not only in the sense that it forgives us from sin, though it certainly does that, but in the sense that it enables us to come near to God, to enter his presence, to enter his sanctuary. Christ came, Paul says in verse 17, "and preached peace to you who were far off and peace to those who were near."

And here is the critical statement (v. 18): "For through him we both have access in one Spirit to the Father." This is the central message of the gospel—we sinners who were far off now have access to the presence of God in one Spirit by grace through faith in the sacrificial atonement of Jesus Christ. This is the gospel, but don't miss the essential connection between this gospel message and the church's worship. Do you see the flow of Paul's thoughts here? We sinners were far off; we were unable to draw near to the sanctuary of God's presence. But now, in the Spirit, through Christ, we have access. We can draw near. "So then," verse 19 says, "you are no longer strangers and aliens [those prohibited from entering the sanctuary of God's presence], but you are fellow citizens with the saints and *members of the household of God.*" There's that phrase again that describes the temple. Notice how he continues to build this imagery of the New Testament temple, the church: "built on the *foundation* of the apostles and prophets, Christ Jesus himself being the *cornerstone*, in whom the whole *structure*, being joined together, grows into a *holy temple* in the Lord. In him you also are being *built* together into a *dwelling place* for God by the Spirit" (vv. 20–22).

Do you see the essential connection between the gospel and worship? Yes, the gospel forgives us from the penalty of sin, but the emphasis here in Ephesians 2 is on having access to the presence of God. The goal of the gospel is to enable us to draw near to the presence of God, in his house, in his temple, where we are then able to fellowship with him, to commune with him. That's the nature of what we're doing when we gather as the church for corporate worship.

This reminds me of one of my favorite passages in the New Testament, Hebrews 10:19–22:

> Therefore, brothers, since we have confidence to enter the holy places by the blood of Jesus,

by the new and living way that he opened for us through the curtain, that is, through his flesh, and since we have a great priest over the house of God, let us draw near with a true heart in full assurance of faith, with our hearts sprinkled clean from an evil conscience and our bodies washed with pure water.

Here, too, the author is deliberately using Old Testament worship language to describe the nature of the gospel—*holy places*, *curtain*, *high priest*—and he says that it is because of Jesus's sacrifice, and because he is our high priest, that we are able to "draw near." There's that phrase again that signifies entering God's presence for communion with him.

Here's the bottom line: the goal of the gospel is to form a temple where God's people meet with him, and that is what we are primarily doing when we gather for corporate worship.

Covenant Renewal in Corporate Worship

Now, this understanding of the purpose of corporate worship being communion with God in his temple—or better yet *as* his temple, the church, which is made possible only through Christ by the Spirit—has important implications for what we do when we gather for corporate worship.

First, corporate worship is for believers. Only those who have access to God, those are brought near through Christ, are members of the household of God and part of the temple. Only believers can commune with God. Therefore, the primary purpose of the corporate worship gathering is for believers to meet with God. Now, this does not mean that we forbid unbelievers from being there. As Paul mentions in 1 Corinthians 14, believers gathering to meet with God is profoundly evangelistic. But when unbelievers come, they come as observers, not as participants, and never do we design what takes place in the corporate church gatherings based on what unbelievers want, any more than what took place in Israel's temple was based on what uncircumcised pagans wanted. Corporate worship is for believers to meet with God.

Second, corporate worship is relational. We don't simply go through a series of rituals as a duty. What we do when we gather is for the purpose of fostering our relationship with God. This is the emphasis of Ephesians 2; this whole passage that leads up to a description of God building a temple by his Spirit expresses those realities in relational terms. The gospel that results in this temple is not simply a legal transaction or ticket to heaven, it is a reconciliation of our relationship with God. We have access to God through Christ, we are welcome in his presence, and so we gather to develop that relationship.

This leads to a third point: corporate worship is formational. Even as believers who have access to God through Christ, members of God's household, our relationship with God is not perfect, it is still growing and deepening. We must continually work to nurture a right relationship with God, allow his Word to correct us, and work toward sanctifying our responses toward him. We certainly do this through personal Bible study and prayer, but one significant and necessary purpose of corporate worship is to help mature our relationship with God. This point is another reason we make sure that the content and forms of our worship are derived from Scripture, because we know that it is inspired Scripture that is profitable for teaching, for reproof, for correction, and for training in righteousness (2 Tim. 3:16).

But also, more specifically, it is the gospel itself that continues to sanctify us. Paul says in Titus 2:11, "For the grace of God has appeared, bringing salvation for all people,"—so he's talking about the gospel that brings salvation, but then notice what else he says the gospel does: "training us to renounce ungodliness and worldly passions, and to live self-controlled, upright, and godly lives in the present age" (v. 12). In other words, the gospel that saved us is also the gospel that sanctifies us—the gospel that reconciled us to God, that brought us near to him, is the gospel that will continue to grow our relationship with him. We don't just believe the gospel for salvation and then leave it behind; even as believers, we must continually renew ourselves in the gospel so that it continues to train us and cultivate our relationship with God. This is the fourth point: corporate worship renews us in the gospel. Historically, Christians have often referred to corporate worship as covenant renewal. It is a way that, as believers, we can weekly renew our covenant relationship with God.

Really, the image of a marriage perfectly depicts this (and, of course, the New Testament also uses marriage as a fitting metaphor for the relationship between Christ and his church). A man and a woman commit to one another in a wedding; this is akin to our salvation when God makes a commitment to save us out of his great love, and we make a commitment to love and serve him. Baptism can be compared to our wedding vows, where we formalize the covenant relationship. So now the man and woman are married; that doesn't change until death parts them.

But the quality of the relationship between a husband and wife rises and falls over time, does it not? Many things can harm the relationship, and many things can rekindle the relationship. Your personal devotional life is like a husband and wife having conversations with each other; that's important to nurture the relationship. But another thing that some couples do to rekindle their relationship is renew their wedding vows. Sometimes they even dress up again like they did when they were first wed, and they repeat those same vows to each other. They're already married; those vows don't "get them married" again. But by repeating their vows, they renew their love for each other and rekindle the relationship.

Corporate worship is like renewing our gospel vows to Christ. Just like when we were first converted, God calls us to draw near to him. Just like at our conversion, we respond with confession of sin and acknowledgment that we have broken God's laws. Just like when we were first saved, we hear words of pardon from God because of the sacrifice of Christ. Just like when we began our relationship with God, we eagerly listen to his instructions and commit to obey. We are not getting "re-saved" each week, but we are renewing our covenant vows to the Lord, and in so doing, we are rekindling our relationship with him and our commitment to him, and he with us.

In the last chapter, I outlined the historic order of worship that derives from Scripture. That particular order was modeled for us specifically because it rehearses the gospel—it allows us, week in and week out, to renew our vows to Christ and rekindle our communion with him.

In our church, we use the following headings to designate our order of worship:

- Revelation
- Adoration
- Confession
- Propitiation
- Proclamation
- Dedication
- Supplication
- Communion
- Commission

These headings identify the order of the gospel, and since our services are structured this way, our corporate worship is a weekly covenant renewal that will help to continually grow our fellowship with God.

This recognition is important for us as we approach what we are doing in corporate worship each week. We need to recognize that what we are doing is not just expressing what is already in our hearts, it is reforming our hearts, renewing our relationship with God each week. So, for example, you might not feel like expressing a certain sentiment in a particular hymn that we're singing one week, but that's not the point; that hymn was chosen to help you renew certain aspects of your relationship with God. Or we might get to the corporate prayer of confession one week, and you might think, well that prayer doesn't really reflect what is in my heart and mind right now, but that's not the point; that prayer was chosen to help remind you of what you are because of the gospel and to help you renew your thankfulness toward God and your commitment to him. Sometimes we say "I love you" to a spouse because we really feel it deeply, but sometimes we say it just to help rekindle the relationship. The same is true for worship. German theologian Dietrich Bonhoeffer once said, "It is not your love that sustains the marriage, but . . . the marriage that sustains your love."[1] The feelings rise and fall, come and go, but the covenant a man and a woman make to one another sustains them despite their fickle feelings. And in the same way, it is not deep feeling for God that sustains our worship, it is what we do when we gather for worship that sustains our love for God.

All of this leads us to conclude and to affirm: the goal of corporate worship is communion with God. Through the gospel, we are God's temple, his house, where we are

---

[1] Dietrich Bonhoeffer, *Letters and Papers from Prison* (Princeton, NJ: Touchstone, 1997), 43.

enabled to meet with him for fellowship. Our primary goal is not evangelism, though a gospel-shaped service will be evangelistic; our primary goal is not expression, though we certainly express toward God in worship; our primary goal is not an emotional experience, though we will certainly feel emotions. Our primary goal is to nurture and cultivate a life of communion with God.

The climax of this covenant-renewal worship is communion around the Lord's Table. Throughout Scripture (and, indeed, history), the ultimate expression of free and open access is being invited to sit at the table. This is illustrated throughout the Old Testament, it is pictured with the table of showbread in the temple, and it is one of the beautiful images depicted by the Lord's Supper. A Christian worship service shows that believers are brought near through Christ, and now sitting around his table both commemorates the sacrifice that made that possible *and* expresses our unity with him and with other Christians as the body of Christ. It does not accomplish peace with God; rather, it is a beautiful expression of the peace already achieved through the sacrifice of Christ and a renewal of our fellowship with him. The Table is the ultimate climax of any gospel-shaped worship service. In the Table, Christians are enabled to sit in full communion with their sovereign Lord because of Christ. The Lord's

Table is the most beautiful earthly enactment of the complete fellowship made possible by union with Christ.

So, we come to corporate worship not to perform rituals out of duty, not primarily to evangelize unbelievers, not even to express what is already in our hearts. We come to corporate worship to meet with God and renew our communion with him.

3

Corporate Worship's Structure: Dialogue with God

Each chapter in this book builds on the previous chapters. The first chapter established the bedrock foundation for all theology and practice of worship: the inspired, inerrant, authoritative, and sufficient Word of God. Chapter 2 showed that God's Word leads us to understand the goal of worship, communion with God. God's Word also helps us to understand the nature of that communion, which will be the focus of this chapter.

Living Water

Jesus's encounter with the Samaritan woman in John 4 is another text that helps us more fully explore what we explored in the last chapter, that worship is communion with God. As with Ephesians 2, the gospel and worship are closely linked. Notice how Jesus begins his conversation with the woman about the gospel by using an image of drinking water:

> A woman from Samaria came to draw water. Jesus said to her, "Give me a drink." (For his disciples had gone away into the city to buy food.) The Samaritan woman said to him, "How is it that you, a Jew, ask for a drink from me, a woman of Samaria?" (For Jews have no dealings with Samaritans.) (John 4:7–9)

Remember the distinction we saw in the last chapter from Ephesians 2 between the clean and unclean, between the circumcised and the uncircumcised, between those able to draw near and those who are far off—those contrasts are illustrated perfectly in this narrative. Here was Jesus, a Jewish male, speaking to a woman of Samaria—that just didn't happen. The relationship between Jews and Samaritans was broken; a deep chasm separated them. Jews would normally take a long trek around Samaria to get from the south of Israel to the north, but here is Jesus going straight through, already picturing the kind of restored communion he was bringing, which Ephesians 2 later explains:

> But now in Christ Jesus you who once were far off have been brought near by the blood of Christ. For he himself is our peace, who has made us both one and has broken down in his flesh the dividing wall of hostility by abolishing the law of commandments expressed in ordinances, that he might create in himself one new man in place of the two, so making peace, and might reconcile us both to God in one body through the cross, thereby killing the hostility. And he came and preached peace to you who were far off and peace to those who were near. For through him we both have access in one Spirit to the Father. So then you are no longer strangers and aliens, but you are fellow citizens with the saints and members of the household of God. (Eph. 2:13–19)

And then notice how he directs the conversation with this Samaritan woman:

> Jesus answered her, "If you knew the gift of God, and who it is that is saying to you, 'Give me a drink,' you would have asked him, and he would have given you living water." The woman said to him, "Sir, you have nothing to draw water with, and the well is deep. Where do you get that living water? Are you greater

than our father Jacob? He gave us the well and drank from it himself, as did his sons and his livestock." Jesus said to her, "Everyone who drinks of this water will be thirsty again, but whoever drinks of the water that I will give him will never be thirsty again. The water that I will give him will become in him a spring of water welling up to eternal life." The woman said to him, "Sir, give me this water, so that I will not be thirsty or have to come here to draw water." (John 4:10–15)

Here, of course, Jesus is playing on the metaphor of water to communicate the nature of a saving relationship with him. The woman thought he was speaking of physical thirst, but he redirected the conversation to her spiritual thirst and her longing for spiritual satisfaction. God created us to commune with him, to find complete satisfaction in him alone. The very nature of sin is rejecting God as the true source of satisfaction and looking to other sources. Jesus highlights this in the life of the woman:

Jesus said to her, "Go, call your husband, and come here." The woman answered him, "I have no husband." Jesus said to her, "You are right in saying, 'I have no husband'; for you have had five husbands, and the one you now have is not your husband. What you have said is true." (John 4:16–18)

God has designed us to long for a satisfying relationship that only he can provide, but sinners desperately try to find that satisfaction in other sources. This woman had gone through five husbands looking for a relationship that would satisfy that longing. Others look to material possessions or influence or success or other earthly relationships to quench the thirst that only a relationship with God can. As Jeremiah said,

> For my people have committed two evils: they have forsaken me, the fountain of living waters, and hewed out cisterns for themselves, broken cisterns that can hold no water. (Jer. 2:13)

This is the image Jesus draws on in his conversation with the woman. He offers her living water—a source of refreshment and satisfaction that will never run dry, a "spring of water welling up to eternal life" (v. 14). Jesus would later say in John 6:35, "I am the bread of life; whoever comes to me shall not hunger, and whoever believes in me shall never thirst." "If anyone thirsts," he called out to the people in John 7:37, "let him come to me and drink." Jesus Christ is the only one who can truly satisfy your thirst for a deep, abiding relationship.

The gospel frees us from the penalty of sin and secures us a home in heaven, but it accomplishes far more than that—the gospel restores fellowship with God and renews our hearts to find satisfaction in him above all else.

Dialogue with God

This passage from John goes on to explain the nature of this all-satisfying communion with God. After Jesus uncovers the fact that the woman is seeking satisfaction in sources that cannot satisfy, the conversation shifts to worship. This might seem like a completely different subject, but it actually continues the discussion by allowing Jesus to explain the nature of the kind of communion with God that both satisfies the thirsty soul and brings honor to him:

> The woman said to him, "Sir, I perceive that you are a prophet. Our fathers worshiped on this mountain, but you say that in Jerusalem is the place where people ought to worship." Jesus said to her, "Woman, believe me, the hour is coming when neither on this mountain nor in Jerusalem will you worship the Father. You worship what you do not know; we worship what we know, for salvation is from the Jews. But the hour is coming, and is now here, when the true worshipers will worship the Father in spirit

and truth, for the Father is seeking such people to worship him. God is spirit, and those who worship him must worship in spirit and truth." The woman said to him, "I know that Messiah is coming (he who is called Christ). When he comes, he will tell us all things." Jesus said to her, "I who speak to you am he." (John 4:19–26)

We will explore the idea of worshiping in spirit and truth more deeply in a later chapter, but for our purposes here, I want to emphasize the two-part structure of this worship—spirit *and* truth. These two elements are essentially connected grammatically; without one, you cannot have the other.[1] You cannot simply worship in spirit, and neither can you simply worship in truth. God is seeking those who will worship him in spirit *and* truth.

What, then, is Jesus communicating here by describing this twofold structure of worship? First, Jesus is at least implying a Trinitarian basis for true worship. We already saw this in Ephesians 2:18—"For through him [Christ] we both have access in one Spirit to the Father." Jesus is alluding to something similar here when he says that the *Father* is seeking those who will worship him in spirit and truth. The term *spirit* here is a word that simply means

---

1 In Greek, there is only one definite article ("the"), not two, signifying that "spirit and truth" are one interconnected idea.

breath. In a moment, we will focus on the primary meaning of this term in this context, but the word can also refer to the Holy Spirit, another member of the Trinity. While the term *truth* refers to God's revelation, remember what Jesus said of himself in John 14:6. He declares, "I am the way, and the *truth,* and the life," so he is at least partially alluding to himself here with the word "truth." The nature of the gospel *and* the nature of true worship is by necessity dependent on the tri-unity of God. We come *to* the Father *through* the Son *in* the Spirit.

The other importance of recognizing the Trinitarian essence of worship is the fact that each member of the Trinity has a relationship with the other members, and when we are converted, we are brought near by the blood of Christ to join that relationship. Jesus communicates this later in John 17 when he prays to the Father that those who believe in him "may be one even as we are one, I in them and you in me, that they may become perfectly one" (vv. 22–23)—once again, this is relationship language to describe the nature of the gospel and the nature of worship as communion with God through the Son in the Spirit.

But then the final idea Jesus is communicating with the phrase "spirit and truth" leads us to a critical related point about the nature of communion with God. This phrase emphasizes the *dialogical* structure of worship.

Worship that is communion between God and his people is not a monologue but a dialogue. God speaks (truth), and his people respond (spirit). While the term *spirit* may imply the Holy Spirit here, the word can also refer to our inner spirits, and in the context of this passage, that seems to be Jesus's primary point. The woman asks him about the proper outward physical place and method for worship, but Jesus emphasizes that in addition to the truth of God's revelation, the inward response of our spirits is necessary for true worship. So, let's unpack this two-part, dialogical structure of worship.

God Is Seeking Worshipers

First, God speaks. One of the most remarkable statements Jesus makes in this conversation is found at the end of verse 23: "The Father is seeking such people to worship him." If worship is communion with God, who initiates that communion? Do we? No. Romans 3 says that "no one seeks for God.... Not even one." We are not the seekers; God is the seeker. He initiates the relationship and calls us to draw near in communion with him through his Son in his Spirit.

Left to ourselves, we would never seek God. We would continue to seek satisfaction in broken cisterns that can hold no water (Jer. 2:13). But God's words have the power to create life. As Paul says in 2 Corinthians 4:6, "for God, who said, 'Let light shine out of darkness,' has shone in our hearts to give the light of the knowledge of the glory of God in the face of Jesus Christ." With just his words, God spoke the universe into existence, and with just his words, God speaks life into dead hearts, causing us to seek him as the source of all-satisfying communion. And so, worship without God's words is impossible.

We Respond

Only after God has spoken his words to us do we respond to him. Worship is not only hearing God's truth; it is also responding to him with our spirits—with our hearts. Worship is not a monologue; it is not simply God speaking to us, though it must begin there. Communion with God necessarily involves our spirits responding to God's truth. Jesus is emphasizing the inward, immaterial part of our being with the term "spirit." Our inner spirits respond to God's truth in communion with he who is spirit. We hear him speak to us through his Word, and then our hearts respond. That is the dialogue of worship.

But neither is worship monological from our side; worship is not simply "performing" for God—that is what characterizes pagan worship. There is some deity out there, and the worshipers want to get his attention to either appease his wrath or receive some sort of blessing, and so they perform before the god. Like Baal's prophets on Mount Carmel, they dance and sing and perform all sorts of rituals to please their god. However,

> their idols are silver and gold, the work of human hands. They have mouths, but do not speak; eyes, but do not see. They have ears, but do not hear; noses, but do not smell. They have hands, but do not feel; feet, but do not walk; and they do not make a sound in their throat. (Ps. 115:4 –7)

False gods don't talk back. This is monological worship.

Unfortunately, some Christians approach worship this way. We think we are the ones initiating the worship, and we pray and invite God to come down and join us. And we have a whole worship service consisting of us performing before the Lord with very little, if any, words from God. I've even heard some Christians say that too much Scripture reading gets in the way of the worship experience. This, too, is monological worship. Actually, it is not worship at all.

In true dialogical worship, we do not invite God to come down to us; God calls us to draw near to him. God speaks first; only then do we respond back to him. And even our responses should be framed by the words, forms, and affections ordained for us by God in his Word, not simply the natural, authentic expressions of our hearts. Our natural, "authentic" responses are often immature, undeveloped, fickle, sometimes even sinful, and in need of reform. Corporate worship is the means through which God forms our image of him and matures our responses toward him.

As we discussed in the last chapter, communing with God is like eating with someone around your dining room table. In that kind of setting, you can let your guard down; there's no need for pretense. Dining with someone is an opportunity for you to listen to them, to get to know them, to enjoy their company. It is an opportunity to share your heart, to communicate something of yourself. There is a mutual give and take that happens around a table. You listen as the other person speaks, and then you respond in dialogue with that person. As you do, your relationship with that person grows deeper as you get to know them better.

This should describe the nature of our relationship with God: conversing with him. We listen intently as he speaks to us through his inspired Word. Our goal in listening to his words is not simply to gain more knowledge;

our goal is to know him better, to learn his likes and his dislikes, to enjoy his company. And then we speak back to him; we tell him how much we love and adore him; we share something of ourselves and cast our burdens on him. And as we share this communion, our relationship with God grows deeper. This is why worship is profoundly relational; all true worship is communion with God, but that communion is not mystical, it's not an energy we feel or a trance that we enter. Communion with God is a conversation, a dialogue.

Dialogue with God in Corporate Worship

Historically, church worship services have been designed in such a way as to both display and nurture this kind of communion by being structured as a dialogue. God speaks, we respond. The worship guide for the church I served in Fort Worth for a decade uses subtitles to help signify the dialogical nature of worship:

- Revelation: God calls us to worship him.
- Adoration: We exalt our glorious God.
- Confession: God calls us to confess our sins. We confess our sins to God.
- Propitiation: God declares us forgiven through Christ. We praise God for our salvation.

- Proclamation: God speaks to us through his Word.
- Dedication: We respond to God's Word.
- Supplication and Communion: God invites us into his presence. We draw near to God.
- Commission: God sends us forth to serve him.

As we saw in the last chapter, this structure follows the logic of the gospel, allowing us to renew our covenant vows to the Lord, but it also follows the shape of conversing with God. And so, let's take a few moments to consider a bit more deeply the elements of our worship from this dialogical perspective.

God's Words to Us

First, it is important that God initiates worship—he begins the conversation. Again, God is seeking worshipers, and so our services should always begin with a call to worship from the Word of God. He is inviting us to draw near to him with true hearts in full assurance of faith; only then do we respond with our part.

Second, our corporate worship must be filled with abundant Scripture. Worship without God's words is impossible. In each major section of a gospel-shaped worship service, we should always first hear from God's Word. God calls us to worship through his Word; God reminds us of our sinfulness and unworthiness to be in his presence through his Word; God declares us forgiven in Jesus Christ through his Word; God speaks to us, corrects us, encourages us, and teaches us through his Word; God invites us to his Table and to his throne of grace in his Word; and God sends us out with his blessing through his Word. One of the central characteristics of Scripture-regulated, communion-driven, dialogical worship is abundant Scripture reading.

Third, even many of the songs we sing are God's words to us. Songs are also our response to God, but many hymns are either direct quotations of God Word or clearly based on God's Word. Sometimes the first hymn of the service, for example, might reveal something about God to us, or we might have a hymn that calls us to confession or proclaims to us forgiveness in Christ. Often the final hymn of commission functions as God's words of charge and blessing as he sends us back into the world.

Fourth, attention to God's words means that we will emphasize the centrality of the preached Word. God speaks to us many times throughout the service, whenever we read or sing his Word, but the sermon is the time when we give focused attention to God's instructions for us. Preaching must always be Word-centered; a sermon is not a self-help presentation or an inspirational lecture; it is not the preacher's clever ideas or opinions. A sermon must always be the exposition of God's Word since it is the Word of God that is alive and powerful to change us.

The final element of corporate worship is also God speaking to us; in this case, his benediction to us. The service begins with God's Word and the service ends with God's Word. From beginning to end, dialogical worship must be thoroughly permeated with God's Word.

Our Words to God

Dialogical worship also contains elements that are responsive—our words back to God as expressions of our spirits. Again, in each major section of a gospel-shaped worship service, we should always respond to God after we hear from him. We respond with praise and adoration after God calls us to worship; we respond with individual and corporate confession after God reminds us of our sin; we respond with thanksgiving and praise after God declares us forgiven in Christ; we respond with dedication and giving after God instructs us; and we respond with fellowship and supplication after God invites us into his presence. As we will explore in the next chapter, corporate worship is not a spectator sport where we simply watch as other things go on, and it is not even just a time in which we listen to God. Scripture-regulated, communion-driven, dialogical worship contains ample opportunities for us to respond to God's Word.

We shouldn't just have a short opening prayer and closing prayer in our services, as is often the case in modern evangelical worship; our services should be filled with prayers. In fact, again, in each major section of the gospel-shaped service, we should have prayers: prayers of praise, prayers of confession, prayers of dedication, and prayers of supplication. These are the responses of our spirits voiced verbally toward God in response to his Word to us.

And while many songs are God's Word to us, most are more often our responses back to God. In each service of our family's church, we have a hymn of praise, a hymn of confession, a hymn of thanksgiving, and a hymn of dedication. Really, songs are often simply sung prayers. Augustine said, "He who sings, prays twice." Singing is often praying, but by adding music, we give voice to the responses of our spirits in ways that words alone cannot.

But even when we pray or when our songs help us to voice the responses of our hearts, it is still important to remember that the purpose of what we are doing is not merely to express what is already in our hearts. The purpose of corporate worship is to *form* our hearts, to shape our responses toward God, to mature our expressions. And so, the best prayers and songs to God are filled with Scripture; God's Word gives us the language and models for the kinds of responses that are best pleasing to God, give him the most glory, and sanctify us most effectively.

We should also always respond to the preached Word. The sermon is a central time in which we focus on God's instruction to us, and since corporate worship is not a monologue, we must always respond in some way when the Word is preached. If you grew up in certain traditions, you might find it unusual that most Reformed churches do not have an altar call. The altar call is actually a nineteenth-century innovation, and there are several reasons Reformed churches don't have them. One reason is that an altar call can give the impression that only those who "feel convicted" and who "come forward" are responding to the preached Word. On the contrary, in dialogical worship, *all* worshipers respond to God's Word every time it is preached. And so, prayer allows us to respond, and a hymn following the sermon allows us to respond. Those responses will be different depending on the sermon and depending on the person; sometimes we respond with conviction, sometimes with commitment, sometimes with thanksgiving, but we always respond to God's Word.

And then, finally, another way we respond to God's Word is through giving. Giving of our personal money is one way that we respond in worship to the Lord, acknowledging that all good gifts come from him, and giving back to him in support of the ministry of his church. This is why we don't have online giving in our church—giving is an act of dialogical worship. This is also why, even though I am paid bi-weekly, I divide my offerings up so that I give every time we gather. Giving in corporate worship is an important act of dialogical worship.

The structure of our services, the songs we sing, the Scriptures we read, the prayers we pray—everything about our services shapes our minds and our hearts to be the kind of people who will commune in dialogue with God like this, hearing from him in his Word, and responding with our hearts and lives.

4

Corporate Worship's Participants: The Whole Congregation

In the year 365, a council of church leaders met in the city of Laodicea to discuss various problems that had arisen in the churches of the region and decide what to do about them. The fourth century was a time of theological controversy and unrest in the church. Church meetings had become disorderly; heretics like Arius were spreading their false doctrine through propaganda hymns that denied the full deity of Christ. And so, this council, among others, made some decisions to bring order and prevent heterodoxy. But while some of what the council did was good, what ultimately resulted was that, to prevent problems, worship was taken away from the people.

The council decided that only ordained priests would be permitted to read Scripture in the services and only the approved guild of professional singers would be allowed to sing. This was only a local council, but it illustrates a trend that developed among most churches over the next thousand years—worship became the work of priests and professional musicians instead of the whole congregation.

Eventually the language of worship was restricted to Latin, a language few laypeople understood, and worship degraded into a performance of a few select individuals—they would perform the worship acts even if no one was in attendance. A strict distinction between clergy and laity developed wherein the clergy did not trust the illiterate, uneducated masses to worship God appropriately on their own; the clergy offered "perfected" worship on behalf of the people. The quality of worship became measured by the excellence of the music and the aesthetic beauty of the liturgy. While this facilitated the production of some quite beautiful sacred music during the period, it resulted in "worship" becoming mostly what the priests did in the chancel. Eventually this "perfect worship" was often distinctly separate from the nave where the people sat by high rails or even a screen. Church architecture deliberately kept the nave dark and the elevated chancel bright.

By the end of the fourteenth century, members of the congregation rarely participated in the Lord's Supper, and even when they did, the cup was withheld from them, lest some of "Christ's blood" spill on the unclean. Roman worship had moved from the "work of the people" (*leitourgia*) to the work of the clergy. As even Roman Catholic liturgical scholar Joseph Jungmann notes, "the people were devout and came to worship; but even when they were present at worship, it was still clerical worship. . . . The people were not much more than spectators."[1] Worship had become the work of priests on behalf of the people, a belief called *sacerdotalism*.

Hopefully, from what we have already seen from Scripture in this book, you can recognize the inherent biblical problems with what developed. As we see in Ephesians 2, all believers, not just a select few, are brought near to God through Christ in one Spirit; all believers are being joined together into a holy temple in the Lord. And as we see in John 4, all believers are capable of communing with God, hearing him speak from his Word, and responding with our spirits to him. And all believers can nurture and cultivate that communion with God through what we do in corporate worship, this covenant renewal

---

1 Joseph Jungmann, "The State of Liturgical Life on the Eve of the Reformation," in *Pastoral Liturgy* (New York: Herder & Herder, 1962), 67–68.

ceremony where we once again rehearse the realities of the gospel and renew our vows to the Lord.

In this chapter I would like to draw our attention to two important New Testament principles about the nature of the church that emphasize the fact that the whole congregation must actively participate in corporate worship.

The Priesthood of All Believers

First, in 1 Peter 2, the apostle uses the same metaphor of a temple to describe the church as Paul did in Ephesians 2, but he extends it further to make a point that explicitly contradicts the sacerdotalism that would later develop in the medieval church. He says in verse 4, "As you *come to him*"—that phrase has the same root as we saw in Ephesians 2 and Hebrews 10, the idea of drawing near to the presence of God through Christ in the Spirit for communion with him. "As you come to him, a living stone rejected by men but in the sight of God chosen and precious." Like Paul, Peter is using the metaphor of a cornerstone to describe Jesus Christ. The cornerstone of what? Keep reading: "you yourselves like living stones are being built up as a *spiritual house*" (v. 5)—there's that phrase again that refers to the church as God's dwelling place, God's temple. So here Peter is developing the same theological truth about the church as Paul did in Ephesians 2: through Christ in the Spirit we have access to the presence of God for communion with him; in fact, we are being built into a sanctuary of his presence.

But then notice how Peter extends the picture further than Paul did: "to be a holy priesthood, to offer spiritual sacrifices acceptable to God through Jesus Christ" (v. 5). Not only are we a spiritual temple where the worship of God takes place, we are also *a holy priesthood*. And notice that he is not designating church leaders only as a holy priesthood but "you yourselves," all of you who have been brought near by the blood of Christ, who are being built into a temple for the Lord—*all of you* are a holy priesthood who offer spiritual sacrifices to God through Jesus Christ. As Martin Luther said in response to the sacerdotalism of the Roman Catholic Church, "all we who are Christians are priests."[2]

The worship that takes place in God's temple is not reserved for ordained clergy who worship on behalf of the congregation as mediators between them and God. *All believers are priests who have full access to the presence of God and who offer spiritual sacrifices to him.*

---
[2] Martin Luther, *The Babylonian Captivity of the Church* (1520).

All believers are priests, but notice that we offer spiritual sacrifices to God *through Jesus Christ*. We have already looked briefly at Hebrews 10:22, which says, "let us draw near," that idea of coming into the presence of God for communion with him. But the previous verse identifies the basis for being able to draw near to God as priests: "since we have a great priest over the house of God." Jesus Christ is the sacrifice that makes communion with God possible, but he is also the great High Priest who leads us into God's presence. No merely human priest serves as a mediator between God and man; "there is one mediator between God and men, the man Christ Jesus" (1 Tim. 2:5). Jesus Christ is the worship leader who brings us into the presence of God, where we all, as priests, offer spiritual sacrifices to God through him. Therefore, *all* who are in Christ are priests who are able to draw near and offer those sacrifices.

The Work of Ministry

But there is a second biblical reason that all believers should actively participate in corporate worship, and it is connected to the formative purpose of corporate worship. In the last two chapters I have stressed the fact that what we do when we gather for corporate worship is not *only* expression toward God, but rather, corporate worship is a weekly time in which we cultivate our communion with

God through renewing our gospel vows. The Word-centered elements of our worship help to continually sanctify us and mature us in our relationship with God.

In Ephesians 4, Paul continues to discuss this nature and purpose of the church. In particular, he emphasizes the importance of all the members of God's temple working together to accomplish the purpose for which God created the church. Only here, instead of using the temple metaphor, Paul uses the metaphor of a body:

> And he gave the apostles, the prophets, the evangelists, the shepherds and teachers, to equip the saints for the work of ministry, for building up the body of Christ. (Eph. 4:11–12)

Notice that Paul begins by affirming the existence of God-called, set-apart leaders of the church—apostles, prophets, evangelists, shepherds, and teachers. The medieval church was not wrong to insist that some men are especially called out by God and equipped to lead God's people: (1) the twelve apostles and prophets who declared the Word of God before the full Bible was completed and served as the foundation of the church; (2) evangelists, who are church planters like Paul and Barnabas and Silas; and (3) pastors, who teach the Word of God and shepherd his people.

But also notice the purpose of these church leaders. Their purpose is not to minister on behalf of the people, nor is it to worship on behalf of the people. Rather, as Paul says in verse 12, their purpose is "to equip *the saints* for the work of ministry, for building up the body of Christ." That word *saints* is used in the New Testament to connote the set-apart, priestly role of all believers, which is why Paul opens his letter to the Ephesians with "to the saints who are in Ephesus." Since all Christians are saints, all Christians are priests who are able to minister. Church leaders exist to equip those saints for the work of ministry.

Notice that in describing this work of ministry, Paul changes the image of the church from a temple to a body. And the purpose of the ministry of all the saints, is to contribute to the building up of that body. Keep reading in verse 13:

> Until we all attain to the unity of the faith and of the knowledge of the Son of God, to mature manhood, to the measure of the stature of the fullness of Christ, so that we may no longer be children, tossed to and fro by the waves and carried about by every wind of doctrine, by human cunning, by craftiness in deceitful schemes. Rather, speaking the truth in love, we

are to grow up in every way into him who is the head, into Christ. (Eph. 4:13–15)

Again, this highlights the formative purpose of the church generally and corporate worship specifically. We gather so that our communion with God might grow and mature, but this is not an individualistic pursuit. Yes, we can and should nurture our fellowship with God through personal times of Bible reading and prayer throughout the week, but we also need the gathered church for our sanctification, where God-called leaders equip us, and where every member participates in the ministry of building one another up.

For our personal communion with God to deepen and mature as God intends, *we must gather with the church*. We cannot do it on our own. We all need each other, so that "the whole body, joined and held together by every joint with which it is equipped, when each part is working properly, makes the body grow so that it builds itself up in love" (v. 16). It is the whole body together, comprised of many members, that grows together in maturity and communion with God. And so, "Let us consider how to stir up one another to love and good works, not neglecting to meet together, as is the habit of some, but encouraging one another, and all the more as you see the Day drawing near" (Heb. 10:24–25). We gather to stimulate one another in our relationship with God—individually and corporately.

We need each other to grow in our relationship with God because, as Paul further develops in 1 Corinthians 12, the Holy Spirit empowers every member of the church with unique gifts to build up the body. Notice what he says in verse 4:

> Now there are varieties of gifts, but the same Spirit; and there are varieties of service, but the same Lord; and there are varieties of activities, but it is the same God who empowers them all in everyone. To each is given the manifestation of the Spirit for the common good. (1 Cor. 12:4–7)

Then, after he lists different kinds of giftings, he says in verse 11, "All these are empowered by one and the same Spirit, who apportions to *each one individually* as he wills." Giftedness for service within the church is not reserved only for those church leaders whom God has called or for a select few. "To *each* is given the manifestation of the Spirit for the common good." Paul says in verse 12, "For just as the body is one and has many members, and all the members of the body, though many, are one body, so it is with Christ." And just as an eye needs a hand and the head needs the feet, so each of us needs each other, with our unique giftedness, to grow in our relationship with God.

This is true for our Christian lives in general, but it is particularly true for the corporate gatherings of the church, which is exactly how Paul applies the principle in 1 Corinthians 14. In a chapter specifically about what we should be doing in the corporate worship services of our church, Paul emphasizes over and over again the purpose of our services: "In church" (v. 19), "when you come together" (v. 26), Paul says, everything should be done for "upbuilding and encouragement and consolation" (v. 3), to "build up the church" (v. 4). In a worship service, Paul says in verse 26, "Let all things be done for building up." Corporate worship is formational, but it is not individualistic formation, it is corporate formation. And so, every member should be actively involved in corporate worship, for the glory of God, to the benefit of our own individual fellowship with God, and for the building up of the entire body.

SACERDOTALISM IN CONTEMPORARY WORSHIP

Unfortunately, while contemporary evangelical churches don't necessarily suffer from the kind of sacerdotalism that developed in the medieval church, a similar problem has emerged. In much contemporary worship today, congregational participation is minimized by the emphasis on performed music on a stage. Like clergy in medieval worship, musicians in contemporary worship have taken on a "priestly" role in the service. Even the title "worship leader" to describe the chief musician developed from the idea that musicians lead the congregation into the presence of God through the music. The quality of worship in many churches has become measured by the excellence of the performed music and the atmosphere it creates. This has resulted in "worship" becoming mostly what the praise team does on the stage, which is separated by bright lights from the darkened congregation. The people have become mere spectators of the worship performed by the praise team on their behalf.

Because of that, today most Christians conceive of their communion with God as something very personal and individualistic. This is exactly what sacerdotalism in the Middle Ages created as well. Since the priests performed the worship and the people didn't participate, people began to consider their relationship with God as something that happened individualistically as they observed what was going on and hopefully "soaked up" some of the benefits. The same thing happens today in many churches. People think that the purpose of corporate worship is for them to have a personal experience as they watch and listen to others perform.

But Christians in times past would never have conceived of their relationship with God in this way, and as we have seen in several passages, the Bible does not conceive of our relationship with God in this way. Yes, we each have a personal relationship with God through Christ, but that relationship is always presented in Scripture as corporate, as many members being built into a body, or as many parts being built into a temple for God.

The Work of the People

This biblical understanding of the corporate importance of gathered worship should impact, therefore, everything we do in corporate worship.

Leaders

First, the Spirit of God does gift individual Christians in unique ways, and he does gift some men as set-apart leaders of the church. The emphasis of this chapter is on every member participating in corporate worship and in the ministry of the church, but that does not discount the fact that God sets aside elders to oversee and shepherd the church and deacons to administrate the physical necessities of the church. In 1 Timothy 3 and Titus 1, Paul gives specific qualifications for elders and deacons, and only some are called to serve in these offices. These are not a special class of Christian, but they are gifted in specific ways by God and charged with leading and equipping God's people, as we saw in Ephesians 4.

But even though elders are the leaders of the church, nothing in the New Testament says that elders are the only ones who can lead various aspects of a corporate worship service, and in fact, as we have seen, the emphasis in several passages is on every member ministering. Nowhere does Scripture say that only elders may read Scripture or pray. Yes, elders should give guidance and leadership to all aspects of the church, but God gifts every church member in a variety of ways, and some of those giftings involve the public reading of Scripture and public prayer. Certainly not everyone has gifts for public speaking, but it isn't limited to just ordained elders.

This is why, in our church, we intentionally include many members of our congregation in public Scripture reading and prayer. If a church member has the ability to speak well in public and has a desire to serve through Scripture reading and prayer in our services, then we welcome their contribution.

Participants

But those instances of public Scripture reading and prayer, or leading and accompanying singing, or preaching the Word are not the only elements of corporate worship. They are certainly aspects of corporate worship that give direction and order to the service, but for the reasons we've seen from Scripture, the whole congregation ought to participate in all aspects of the service. So, let's explore what implications this important principle has for our corporate worship services.

First, a church should not intentionally darken the congregation and light up the front. Again, this was deliberately done through medieval architecture, and it is often done electronically in many contemporary worship services. Making the congregation dark communicates that they are merely spectators watching the worship taking place on the stage. The whole congregation ought to be able to see one another as they all participate in corporate worship.

Second, congregational singing is the most important form of worship music. I do not believe there is anything inherently wrong with a soloist or ensemble or choir, but since Scripture commands the whole congregation to teach *one another* with psalms and hymns and spiritual songs, the whole congregation ought to sing. Especially when a song is a response toward God, we all ought to be responding through that song. Yes, God gifts some people with abilities to sing or play musical instruments, but the whole congregation ought to sing, even if someone doesn't think they've been especially gifted musically.

This also affects the way congregational singing is accompanied. Instrumental accompaniment is meant to support congregational singing, not overpower it. This is why churches have found the organ to be so useful. Since the organ can sustain its sound, it is particularly suited to support congregational singing better than just about any other instrument. But the power of an organ is also a danger, and if the organ is ever so loud, or the accompaniment so complicated, that it overpowers or distracts from congregational singing, something needs to change. Some instruments, while they may be beautiful for playing solos, are not able to support congregational singing. You can't support singing well with a flute. The same is true for a guitar. Those instruments are too soft and cannot sustain sound long enough to be able to support the singing of a congregation, unless they are artificially amplified. The goal should be to do whatever will best help to encourage and support the whole congregation singing.

Third, we should emphasize corporate prayer. In most churches, prayers are offered by an individual, but we should never have the idea that the person is praying on our behalf and we are simply spectators. If someone leads in a prayer, we should actively engage our minds and hearts with that prayer, making the prayer our own. And this is one reason we frequently have corporate prayers, whether corporate prayers of praise or our weekly corporate prayer of confession. Every week, the whole congregation ought to be actively participating in corporate prayer. We even intentionally include extemporaneous corporate prayers of praise and intercession in our services. All these examples help to ensure that we *all* are responding to the Lord in prayer, not just a select few.

Fourth, the whole congregation should read Scripture. Sometimes an individual will read Scripture publicly in a service, but frequently we include public Scripture readings that involve the whole congregation. The Word of God is available to all believers, so all believers can and should publicly read and affirm what God has said.

Fifth, as I mentioned briefly in the last chapter, all believers should respond to the Word of God every time it is preached. Those responses will vary from person to person, but we all respond in some way through prayer, a hymn of response, and our giving, not just certain people who "feel" convicted.

And then, finally, participation of the whole congregation is another important and beautiful benefit of the Lord's Table as the climax of our corporate worship gatherings. The Lord's Table illustrates our communion with God through Christ. It is a way to renew our vows to him, but we don't come to the Table as individuals. We come together as members of one body and surround the Table of the Lord. And in so doing, we portray and reaffirm that our union with Christ is corporate. "Because there is one bread," Paul says in 1 Corinthians 10:17, "we who are many are one body, for we all partake of the one bread."

5

Corporate Worship's Essence: Spiritual Response

One of the clearest ways you can determine someone's fundamental theology of worship is to ask them the following question: "How do you know that you have worshiped?" If, as we have discussed in this book, we are the temple of God's Spirit and our goal in worship is to commune with God, how do we know we have accomplished our goal? How do we know we have worshiped?

In this chapter, I would like to tie everything together as we seek to answer this fundamental question: What is the true essence of our worship?

In the book of Colossians, Paul confronts the heretical teaching that defined the essence of a true relationship with Christ in terms of external rituals and requirements. Apparently, some were teaching that certain physical regulations were essential to Christianity, but Paul insists that the believers in Colossae should not be taken captive by these empty philosophies that were according to human tradition and not according to Christ (2:8). He says that these "have indeed an appearance of wisdom" (2:23), but they are not from God and do not define the essence of our relationship with him.

Instead, Paul begins chapter 3 by explaining the true essence of our relationship with God through Christ.

> If then you have been raised with Christ, seek the things that are above, where Christ is, seated at the right hand of God. Set your minds on things that are above, not on things that are on earth. For you have died, and your life is hidden with Christ in God. When Christ who is your life appears, then you also will appear with him in glory. (Col. 3:1–4)

We will look more closely in a moment at what Paul is arguing here, but notice that Paul is essentially distinguishing between the heavenly and the earthly, between the spiritual and the physical, and he insists that the essence of our relationship with God is heavenly; the essence of our communion with God is spiritual.

This does not mean, however, that physical, earthly matters are unimportant. Notice what Paul commands specifically for the corporate gatherings of the church beginning in verse 16:

> Let the word of Christ dwell in you richly, teaching and admonishing one another in all wisdom, singing psalms and hymns and spiritual songs, with thankfulness in your hearts to God. And whatever you do, in word or deed, do everything in the name of the Lord Jesus, giving thanks to God the Father through him. (Col. 3:16–17)

So, what is Paul saying here about the relationship between the spiritual and the physical in our fellowship with God? Let's look first at what he says about the physical, embodied expressions of corporate worship.

Embodied Expressions of Corporate Worship

As physical beings, much of what we do in corporate worship is embodied. Here in Colossians 3, we find a command to sing—the Greek word translated as "singing" literally means "make a melody with the vocal cords." That may seem obvious, but some Christians in times past have argued that this passage refers to singing internally, not externally. No, we are supposed to sing with our voices in corporate worship. We cannot teach and admonish *one another* with singing unless we use our physical voices to do so. Likewise, Paul says in Ephesians 5:19, "addressing one another"—you can't do that with internal singing—"in psalms and hymns and spiritual songs, singing and making melody to the Lord with your heart." The word *singing* there is the same as in Colossians 3, but he also adds the word translated as "making melody," which literally means "to pluck a stringed instrument." So, clearly, the music of our corporate worship is a physical, audible expression.

We also necessarily use our bodies in other ways in corporate worship, don't we? To let the Word of Christ richly dwell within us, as Paul commands in this text, we must use our eyes and voices to physically read the Scriptures. We use our ears to listen as others speak and sing. We even use our mouths and fingers as we eat and drink at the Lord's Table. We cannot worship God corporately according to his instructions without the use of our bodies.

Indeed, the Bible teaches that the human body is good. God created the body and, therefore, by nature the body is good. Furthermore, Jesus Christ took on a human body at his incarnation, and he will have that body for the rest of eternity. Jesus died bodily, and he was raised bodily from that death. He ascended bodily into heaven, and one day he will return to the earth in his body. Job affirmed, "For I know that my Redeemer lives, and at the last he will stand upon the earth" (Job 19:25). The Bible teaches that God, through Christ, has saved our souls, but he has also saved our bodies (1 Thess. 5:23).

Some Christians in the first couple centuries of the church adopted a Platonic philosophy that believed the body to be inherently evil. This resulted in what is known as the Gnostic heresy, which denied that Jesus Christ really had a physical body or that he rose bodily from the grave. Gnosticism also taught that we must try to completely free ourselves from our bodies by denying our bodies what we need to survive physically and instead attempt to become one with God's spiritual essence. This heresy is specifically what Paul was addressing here in Colossians as well as in other letters, such as in 1 Timothy when he said that Jesus "was manifested in the flesh" (3:16) and that "everything created by God is good" (4:4). And John explicitly condemned Gnosticism when he said, "For many deceivers have gone out into the world, those who do not confess the coming of Jesus Christ in the flesh" (2 John 1:7). Orthodox theologians continued to fight against this heresy until it was officially condemned in the fourth century. The body was created by God, Christ took on human flesh, and therefore the body is good, and our corporate worship is embodied worship.

This embodied reality of corporate worship is one reason that we must physically meet together. We cannot sing to one another without physically being together. The New Testament frequently emphasizes the importance of meeting together. John said in 2 John 1:12, "Though I have much to write to you, I would rather not use paper and ink. Instead I hope to come to you and talk face to face, so that our joy may be complete," and he wrote similarly in 3 John. Paul stressed several times to the believers in Rome his desire to be there with them, so that he might enjoy their company and be refreshed together with them (Rom. 15:23–24, 32). He longed to physically gather with the believers in the church at Thessalonica, saying that he "endeavored the more eagerly and with great desire to see you face to face" (1 Thess. 2:17), and he urged Timothy to be diligent to come to him quickly (2 Tim. 4:9). Paul recognized the importance of physically being together for fellowship.

And so, the author of Hebrews commanded, "Do not neglect to meet together." It's why passages about corporate worship in the New Testament frequently emphasize the physical gathering of corporate worship. In 1 Corinthians 11 and 14, Paul repeats the idea multiple times: "when you come together" (11:17), "when you come together as a church" (11:18), "when you come together" (11:20), "when you come together to eat" (11:33), "when you come together" (11:34), "when you come together" (14:26). Corporate worship assumes the necessity of a physical gathering where we do physical things. "Where two or three are gathered in my name," Jesus said, "there am I among them" (Matt. 18:20).

SPIRITUAL ESSENCE OF CORPORATE WORSHIP

Feeling God's spiritual presence in Home/Temple

Yet that very statement leads us to the primary point of this chapter. Jesus said that where two or three are physically gathered in his name, there he is among them, but is Jesus physically in the midst of us when we gather? No, not since he ascended into heaven. Stephen saw Jesus standing at the right hand of God the Father (Acts 7:56). Colossians 3:1 says that Christ is "seated [bodily] at the right hand of God." So, if Jesus is bodily in heaven, and we are gathered bodily here on earth, how can he be in the midst of us?

Notice how the verse opens: "If then you have been raised with Christ." The first point to recognize here is that all who are united with Christ are also seated with him in heaven. Verse 3 alludes to this reality: "For you have died, and your life is hidden with Christ in God." Paul says it even more explicitly in Ephesians 2:6 when he states that God has "raised us up with [Christ] and seated us with him in the heavenly places in Christ Jesus." Christ is seated in heaven, and since we are in him, we are with him there. Remember what Paul says a few verses later in Ephesians 2:18: "For through him we both have access in one Spirit to the Father." We have access to the Father because, in one Spirit through Christ, we are actually there in the presence of God in heaven.

This is a reality, and yet we also recognize that it is not yet a physical reality. Our bodies are still here on earth, while we really are seated with Christ in the heavenly places. What this reveals is the important *spiritual essence* of our relationship with God through Christ. As Paul says, we have access *in one Spirit*. The Spirit of God is the agent who makes this possible because it is a spiritual reality.

This is also part of what Jesus meant in John 4 when he said that God is seeking those who will "worship the Father in spirit and truth" (v. 23). Since "God is spirit" (v. 24) and does not have a body like man, true worship takes place in its essence in the Spirit, which is why it is essential that the Holy Spirit dwell within the New Testament temple—the church—in the same way he dwelt in the temple of the Old Testament. Back then, worship was limited to that physical, Spirit-indwelt temple, but "the hour . . . is now here" (v. 23) that worship takes place wherever two or three Spirit-indwelt believers gather together, for there Christ is "in the midst of them."

While physical expressions are absolutely good and necessary aspects of what we do when we gather for corporate worship, the *essence* of what we are doing is fundamentally spiritual. When we gather, we are doing things physically here on earth, in this place, with one another, but because we are united with Christ, we are actually in God's presence spiritually in heaven. As we have discussed, we are communing with God through Christ when we worship, but we do so in the Spirit; our communion with God is not something that we physically experience or feel—our communion with God is essentially spiritual.

This is why Paul says in Colossians 3 that we must "seek the things that are above, where Christ is, seated at the right hand of God. Set your minds on things that are above, not on things that are on earth" (vv. 1–2). The word translated "mind" here is a word that refers to more than just thinking; it refers to the inner seat of spiritual activity.

That's why the KJV translates this as "set your affection on things above." That nature of our fellowship with God is spiritual in its essence, and so our central focus should not be on things that are on earth, but rather, our inner spirits must be set on the true reality of things that are above, where Christ is, seated at the right hand of God, where we who are in him really are in his presence spiritually.

What Paul said about the church being the temple of God ties in with this reality. As we noted from Ephesians 2, the church is God's temple, the place of his dwelling, but this temple is not a physical location or literal building. It's a spiritual reality. And it's not even that the physical gatherings of the church are God's temple; rather, the true temple is in heaven, and we are spiritually part of that real temple.

This is exactly what Hebrews 8 teaches. The author says, "We have [a perfect] high priest, one who is seated at the right hand of the throne of the Majesty in heaven, a minister in the holy places, in the true tent that the Lord set up, not man" (vv. 1–2). Notice the similar language there of Jesus Christ as one who is seated at the right hand of God, notice that this passage calls him our high priest, and notice the reference to the *true* tent, the *true* temple that exists where he is, in heaven. As Ephesians 2 teaches, we are part of that temple in heaven, but we are part of that temple spiritually, not yet physically.

And so, everything we do physically here on earth as God's temple is a participation with the true worship taking place in the true temple of heaven. The implication then, is that the essence of our communion with God is not physical, but spiritual. We can see this in how Paul discusses singing in Colossians 3. He commands us to verbally sing—to literally make melody with our vocal cords—but the singing itself is not really the essence of our communion with God. Notice how he identifies the essence of what we are doing at the end of verse 16: "with thankfulness in your *hearts* to God." Remember, Paul had commanded at the beginning of the chapter to set our hearts on things that are above, and now he is saying that our physical, verbal singing is an expression of our hearts to God. The physical singing flows out of the essence of our worship—hearts directed toward God. He says something similar in Ephesians 5:19: "singing and making melody *to the Lord with your heart*." The physical act of singing alone is not worship; our physical vocal and instrumental music is to be an expression of the true essence of our worship—hearts directed toward the Lord.

It is important that we recognize the proper function of our physical expressions of worship and the fundamental spiritual essence of worship. The physical expressions themselves are never the essence of our communion with

God; plenty of people do the physical stuff without truly worshiping. Rather, the physical aspects of worship should be an expression of the spiritual responses of our hearts toward God in the true heavenly temple. We cannot be satisfied with just going through the motions, assuming if we sing and pray and read the Bible and listen to a sermon, we have communed with God. No, the essence of true communion with God is in our hearts, hearts set on things above.

The problem is, physical human beings naturally tend toward defining the essence of our communion with God in physical terms. We know that the Bible teaches that we are seated in the heavens with Christ, we know that we are God's temple, we know that we have access to the presence of God through Christ in the Spirit, but we want physical proof of these biblical realities. We want to be able to "feel" God's presence; we want to tangibly experience communion with God. And so, when we're asked how we know that we've worshiped, we want to be able to say something like "I felt God. I experienced his presence."

But here's what we need to remember: while we truly are in God's presence through Christ, it is *in the Spirit*, and it is not yet a physical reality. It will one day be a physical reality. Paul references this in Colossians 3:4 when he says, "When Christ who is your life appears [bodily], then you also will appear [bodily] with him in glory." But that time has not yet come. We are already there spiritually, but not yet bodily.

Worship by Faith, Not Sight

The spiritual essence of worship is why faith is necessary for communion with God in this already/not yet condition. Hebrews 10:22 says, "Let us draw near with a true heart in full assurance of faith." Faith is the means by which we are able to draw near to communion with God through Christ, though we do not yet experience that communion in physical ways. The author of Hebrews defines faith in chapter 11 as "the assurance of things hoped for, the conviction of things not seen" (v. 1). We need faith as we draw near to communion with God because, even though we know we have access to the presence of God in the real temple of heaven, we cannot see it; we cannot see God or feel God or experience God with any of our physical senses. Our communion with God is at its essence spiritual.

And so, we come with assurance and conviction that when we draw near through Christ, we are actually in the presence of God even though we have no tangible, physical proof. When we're asked how we know we've worshiped, we ought to answer: "I know I've worshiped because I drew near to God, through Christ, with a sincere heart in full assurance of faith." Our assurance that we've worshiped is not based on anything physical; it's not based on simply doing our duty, nor is it based on any kind of feeling or experience.

Unfortunately, throughout history, some of God's people have forgotten this necessity of faith and instead have expected the essence of communion with God to be physical. For example, during the Middle Ages some theologians, rightly understanding that Christian worship is participation with the worship of heaven, nevertheless failed to recognize that this is currently something to be accepted in faith as a spiritual reality rather than a physical experience. Medieval Christians wanted to experience the worship of heaven tangibly here on earth, either expecting that heaven came down to them while they worshiped or that they were led into the heavenly temple through the sacramental ceremonies.

Even today, Christians expect to be able to tangibly feel the manifest presence of God when they worship, through a visible display of his glory, miraculous gifts, or emotional rapture. The goal of music and the "worship leader" is to "usher worshipers" into the presence of God in heaven, or as one author put it, to "bring the congregational worshipers into a corporate awareness of God's manifest presence."[1] This has resulted in a new understanding of the place of music in corporate worship, perhaps best described by Ruth Ann Ashton's book, *God's Presence through Music*, raising the matter of musical style to a level of significance that some contemporary worshipers describe as "musical sacramentality." Music is now considered a primary means through which people experience God's presence in worship.

This is a serious misunderstanding of the essence of worship and the role of music in worship. Notice the order of what Paul says in Colossians 3:16. He says first that the Word of Christ should dwell richly within us. We read and hear God's Word, and God's Word dwells within our spirits. This is similar to Ephesians 5:18, where he says, "Be filled [by] the Spirit." Spirit filling and the Word dwelling richly within us are the same thing—the Holy Spirit of God fills us with the Word he inspired. That comes first. Only then do we verbally sing to the Lord as an expression of what the Holy Spirit of God did in our hearts through his Word. Yes, the physical expression of singing is im-

---

[1] Barry Griffing, "Releasing Charismatic Worship," in *Restoring Praise & Worship to the Church* (Shippensburg, PA: Revival, 1989), 92.

portant, but it is a response to the Spirit filling our hearts with his Word, not the way we somehow feel the presence of God. Many Christian worshipers today expect music to do what only the Spirit can do through his Word.

Christian leaders up until the twentieth century universally avoided music in worship that simply worked up intense emotion artificially. They knew that it is too easy to interpret the feelings created by the energy of music as something spiritual. They're not—emotion created by exciting music is just emotion. It's not bad, but it's not the essence of our communion with God, and it is certainly not the felt presence of God. Historically, church leaders have insisted that the music we use in corporate worship be filled with the Word of God and composed in such a way that the music does not manipulate our emotions. Rather, the music should modestly give expression to the affections of our hearts that have been created by the Spirit through his Word richly dwelling within us.

Worship That Cannot Be Touched

All of what we have seen in this series on the fundamentals of corporate worship is captured beautifully at the end of Hebrews 12. We have seen that the authority for our corporate worship is God's revelation. The goal of what we are doing is communion with God. The structure of our communion with God is a dialogue. Every believer is an active participant in this communion. And we have seen that, while we engage in physical expressions in our worship, the essence of our communion with God is spiritual.

In Hebrews 12, the author climaxes the book with a vivid description of our goal: drawing near to God for worship. He begins in verse 18 by describing what we Christians have not come to—what may be touched. In other words, as we have discussed in this chapter, Christian worship is not at its essence physical. But then he highlights the far better spiritual reality—we can't touch our worship because we are worshiping spiritually in heaven:

> But you have come to Mount Zion and to the city of the living God, the heavenly Jerusalem, and to innumerable angels in festal gathering, and to the assembly of the firstborn who are enrolled in heaven, and to God, the judge of all, and to the spirits of the righteous made perfect, and to Jesus, the mediator of a new covenant, and to the sprinkled blood that speaks a better word than the blood of Abel. (Heb. 12:22–24)

We are not worshiping physically in heaven yet, but in Christ we are worshiping there spiritually in a very real sense—we "have come to Mount Zion." With Christ's coming, God no longer has to condescend and enter the fabric of the physical universe to manifest himself to his people; he can now allow us to ascend into heaven itself to worship him, which is superior to the physical earthly worship of the Old Testament. This is possible because of Jesus's mediation on behalf of his people (12:24). We can now approach God with full confidence in worship.

Notice the corporate nature of this worship. We are joining our hearts with the worship around God's throne, comprised of innumerable angels in festal gathering, and the assembly of the firstborn who are enrolled in heaven, and the spirits of the righteous made perfect. This is truly corporate worship.

Also notice the communal nature of this worship. We are coming to God himself, the judge who accepts us because of the sacrifice of his Son. We are coming to Jesus, who has established a covenant with us. And through this worship, we are once again renewing our covenant vows, hearing him as he speaks, and responding with our spirits, further cultivating our relationship with him.

This is what is really happening when we draw near to worship God corporately. We come by faith and not by sight since we are not yet there physically; but one day faith will be sight. Now we gather around Christ's Table to renew our vows, and he is here spiritually, though we cannot see him with physical eyes. One day we will sit at his Table in our physical, glorified bodies, clothed in fine linen, bright and pure, and we will see Christ bodily with our physical eyes. And we will join our physical voices with "the voice of a great multitude, like the roar of many waters and like the sound of mighty peals of thunder, crying out, 'Hallelujah! For the Lord our God the Almighty reigns. Let us rejoice and exult and give him the glory'" (Rev. 19:6–7).

Therefore, let us be grateful for receiving a kingdom that cannot be shaken, and let us offer to God acceptable worship, with reverence and awe, for our God is a consuming fire.

Appendix

Example Covenant Renewal Service Orders

If you want to utilize a gospel shape to your church's worship service, here is a brief summary of how I plan such services based on the biblical principles laid out in this book.

Since worship itself is drawing near to communion with God through Christ in the Spirit by faith, the order of corporate worship should reflect this. Corporate worship shaped by the gospel reminds us weekly of how and why we can draw near in communion with God despite our sin, and it shapes us to live our lives in light of these truths.

Therefore, the order of corporate worship should follow the flow of the gospel. This is how Christians have structured their worship for hundreds of years, and I believe we should continue this practice today. I also believe the structure should reflect worship in "spirit and truth"—that is, corporate worship should be a dialogue in which God speaks to us and then we speak back to him. Finally, worship is "the people's work"—the structure of worship should allow for regular, active participation of the congregation rather than a divide between "performer" and "spectators."

These are the governing principles that determine how I order worship services. Each week the hymns are different, the Scripture readings vary, and the sermon progresses expositionally through books of the Bible, but the "skeleton" of the service always remains the same. The basic structure of the service is the shape of the gospel:

1. Revelation: God reveals himself and calls us to worship.
2. Adoration: We recognize the greatness of God and praise him for it.
3. Confession: When we acknowledge the holiness of God, we also recognize our unworthiness to draw near to him because of our sin.

4. Propitiation: As Christians, we are assured of pardon through the sacrifice of Christ, which makes worship possible.
5. Proclamation: The Word of God is taught.
6. Dedication: We respond to the Word of God with consecration.
7. Supplication: We bring our requests before the Lord.
8. Communion: Celebration of free access to God because of Christ's death on our behalf.
9. Commission: God sends us into the world to serve him. Just as the service began with God's word, it ends with a word of blessing from him.

The service opens with a historic Christian greeting (also known as the "salutation") that sets this apart as a gathering of Christians. The service actually begins, however, with God speaking to us. We do not come to worship of our own initiative, and (contrary to pagan worship and some evangelical emphases as well) we are not somehow "calling God down" or inviting him to join us. Rather, it is God who calls us to draw near to him, and thus the service begins with a scriptural call to worship.

When God reveals himself to us, two responses are inevitable. First, we respond with adoration and praise. This usually takes the form of a hymn, a prayer of praise, and a doxology. Then, we recognize our sin and unworthiness, and so we confess our sins to God. We responded this way when we first believed, and we should continue to do so daily. Thus, through a Scripture reading, a hymn, silent repentance, and a corporate prayer of confession, as a congregation we acknowledge our sin together before God. As Christians, we find forgiveness and pardon in Christ, and so the service continues with celebrating that forgiveness. Through a Scripture affirmation and a hymn of praise for Christ's sacrifice, we both rejoice in the gospel and proclaim it to any unbelievers who may be attending. Next, we are ready to hear God's instructions through the preaching of his Word. Our response is one of consecration and dedication. We then bring our requests for ourselves, our church, and the world to God in corporate prayer.

The climax of the service is Communion. Worship is drawing near to God in communion through Christ, and this is what the whole service has been progressing toward. Coming boldly to the throne of grace (Heb. 4:16) for supplication and eating at God's Table means that we are welcome and that we have open access to him, despite our sin. This is possible only through Christ's sacrifice on the cross, which is beautifully pictured in the Communion elements. Communion with God is the purpose of the gospel, and thus Communion is the climax of a worship service. I actually advocate weekly Communion, although our church does not practice that at this time. The service concludes with a word from God in which he sends us into the world to obey him and share the gospel with unbelievers, along with a word of blessing.

The particular hymns, Scripture passages, and other elements of the service that I choose are determined by their fit in three categories: First, I consider the church year. Our church follows the general Protestant church calendar that remembers the coming, life, death, resurrection, and ascension of Christ. I use a lectionary as a starting point here, but I don't always follow it strictly if the assigned passages don't fit other objectives I have for the service. Second, I consider the function of the hymns or Scripture passages within the liturgy. I pay careful attention to choosing elements that fit the structure of Revelation, Adoration, Confession, Propitiation, Proclamation, Dedication, Supplication, Communion, and Commission, and that also facilitate the dialogue between God and us in the service. Third, I consider the sermon passage and theme for the day. I choose hymns and Scripture passages that both fit the gospel shape and tie into the sermon text, which usually follows a *lectio continua* progress through books of the Bible. Usually, I am able to create a service that connects all three of these categories so that through the course of the church's life, we are formed both by the gospel narrowly (in the weekly liturgy) *and* the "whole counsel of God" broadly (as the songs and texts connect with the *lectio continuo* preaching). This takes a lot of work and a good bit of time, but it is always very rewarding when it all comes together and is, I believe, formative for our church.

On the following pages are a few sample services to help give you an idea of what this might look in your context.

Example 1: Service without the Lord's Table

Revelation: God Calls Us to Worship Him
    Silent Prayer and Meditation
    Prelude: "Guide Me, O Thou Great Jehovah"
    Christian Greeting

        Leader: The Lord be with you.
        People: And also with you.

    Scripture Reading: Isaiah 25:1–9

        Reader: The Word of the Lord.
        People: Thanks be to God.

Adoration: We Exalt Our Glorious God
    Hymn: "Let Us, with a Gladsome Mind"
    Prayer of Praise
    Gloria Patri

Confession: God Calls Us to Confess Our Sins
    Scripture Reading: Psalm 70:4–5
    Hymn: "Come, Ye Sinners"

We Confess Our Sins to God
    Silent Prayers of Repentance

Corporate Prayer of Confession

Have mercy on me, O God,
according to your steadfast love;
according to your abundant mercy
blot out my transgressions.
Wash me thoroughly from my iniquity,
and cleanse me from my sin!
For I know my transgressions,
and my sin is ever before me.
Against you, you only, have I sinned
and done what is evil in your sight,
so that you may be justified in your words
and blameless in your judgment.
Behold, I was brought forth in iniquity,
and in sin did my mother conceive me.
Behold, you delight in truth in the inward being,
and you teach me wisdom in the secret heart.
Purge me with hyssop, and I shall be clean;
wash me, and I shall be whiter than snow.
Hide your face from my sins,
and blot out all my iniquities.
O Lord, open my lips,
and my mouth will declare your praise.
For you will not delight in sacrifice, or I would give it;
you will not be pleased with a burnt offering.
The sacrifices of God are a broken spirit;
a broken and contrite heart, O God, you will not

despise,
through Jesus Christ, our Lord. Amen.

—from Psalm 51

Propitiation: God Declares Us Forgiven through Christ
> Declaration of the Good News: 1 Thessalonians 5:9
>> Leader: In Christ your sins are forgiven you!
>> *People: The Lord be praised!*

We Praise God for Our Salvation
> Hymn: "Sing Praise to God Who Reigns Above"

Proclamation: God Speaks to Us through His Word
> Scripture Reading: 1 Thessalonians 5:23
> Sermon: "What Is Sanctification?"

Dedication: We Respond to God's Word
> Hymn: "Take My Life and Let It Be Consecrated"
> Offertory Prayer
> Offertory

Supplication: We Cast Our Burdens before the Lord
> Intercessory Prayer

Commission: God Sends Us Forth to Serve Him
> Pastoral Welcome and Announcements

Hymn: "Lord, Speak to Me, That I May Speak"
Pastoral Charge and Benediction
Postlude: "Glory Be to God on High"

Example 2: Service with the Lord's Table

Revelation: God Calls Us to Worship Him

Silent Prayer and Meditation
Prelude: "My Inmost Heart Now Raises"
Christian Greeting

Leader: The Lord be with you.
People: And also with you.

Responsive Scripture Reading:
Psalm 145:8–9, 14–21

Leader: The Lord is gracious and merciful, slow to anger and abounding in steadfast love.
People: The Lord is good to all, and his mercy is over all that he has made.
Leader: The Lord upholds all who are falling and raises up all who are bowed down.
People: The eyes of all look to you, and you give them their food in due season.
Leader: You open your hand; you satisfy the desire of every living thing.

People: The Lord is righteous in all his ways and kind in all his works.

Leader: The Lord is near to all who call on him, to all who call on him in truth.

People: He fulfills the desire of those who fear him; he also hears their cry and saves them.

Leader: The Lord preserves all who love him, but all the wicked he will destroy.

People: My mouth will speak the praise of the Lord, and let all flesh bless his holy name forever and ever.

Leader: The Word of the Lord

People: Thanks be to God.

Adoration: We Exalt Our Glorious God
    Hymn: "O Worship the King"
    Prayer of Praise
    Gloria Patri

Confession: God Calls Us to Confess Our Sins
    Scripture Reading: Isaiah 55:1–5

We Confess Our Sins to God
    Silent Prayers of Repentance
    Corporate Prayer of Confession

      Almighty and merciful God,

we have erred and strayed from your ways like
lost sheep.
We have followed too much
the devices and desires of our own hearts.
We have offended against your holy laws.
We have left undone those things which we
ought to have done;
and we have done those things which we ought
not to have done,
and there is no good in us.
O Lord, have mercy upon us.
Spare those who confess their faults.
Restore those who are penitent,
according to your promise declared to the world
in Christ Jesus, our Lord.
And grant, O merciful God, for his sake,
that we may live a holy, just, and humble life
to the glory of your holy name.
Amen.

—from The Book of Common Prayer

Propitiation: God Declares Us Forgiven through Christ

Declaration of the Good News: John 7:37–38

Leader: In Christ your sins are forgiven you!

People: The Lord be praised!

We Praise God for Our Salvation
>Hymn: "I Heard the Voice of Jesus Say"

Proclamation: God Speaks to Us through His Word
>Scripture Reading: 1 John 2:15–18
>Sermon: "Love Not the World"

Dedication: We Respond to God's Word
>Hymn: "O Jesus, I Have Promised"
>Offertory Prayer
>Offertory

Communion: Christ Invites Us to His Table
>Declaration of Faith: Nicene Creed
>Introduction and Welcome
>Prayer of Thanksgiving
>Words of Institution
>The Acclamation
>
>>Leader: Great is the mystery of our faith!
>>
>>*People: Christ has died! Christ is risen! Christ will come again! Hallelujah!*
>
>Hymn: "Praise God from Whom All Blessings Flow"
>Benevolence Offering

Commission: God Sends Us Forth to Serve Him
>Pastoral Welcome and Announcements

Hymn: "A Charge to Keep I Have"
Pastoral Charge and Benediction
Postlude: "Blest Be the Tie that Binds"

Example 3: Service Based on Isaiah 6

God Calls Us to Worship

Scripture Reading: Isaiah 6:1–4

We Praise God

Hymn: "Holy, Holy Holy"
Corporate Prayer of Praise

We praise you, O God; we acclaim you as Lord;
all creation worships you, the Father everlasting.
To you all angels, all the powers of heaven,
the cherubim and seraphim, sing in endless praise:
Holy, holy, holy Lord, God of power and might,
heaven and earth are full of your glory.
The glorious company of apostles praise you.
The noble fellowship of prophets praises you.
The white-robed army of martyrs praise you.
Throughout the world the holy church acclaims you:
Father, of majesty unbounded;
your true and only Son, worthy of all praise;
the Holy Spirit, advocate and guide.
You, Christ, are the King of glory,
the eternal Son of the Father.

When you took our flesh to set us free,
you humbly chose the virgin's womb.
You overcame the sting of death
and opened the kingdom of heaven to all believers.
You are seated at God's right hand in glory.
We believe that you will come to be our judge.
Come, then, Lord, and help your people,
bought with the price of your own blood,
and bring us with your saints
to glory everlasting. Amen.

—based on the fourth-century Latin hymn "Te Deum Laudamus"

God Calls Us to Confession

Scripture Reading: Isaiah 6:5

We Confess Our Sins

Hymn: "When I Survey the Wondrous Cross"
Silent Prayers of Repentance
Corporate Prayer of Confession

Out of the depths I cry to you, O Lord!
O Lord, hear my voice!
Let your ears be attentive to the voice of my pleas for mercy!
If you, O Lord, should mark iniquities,
O Lord, who could stand?

> But with you there is forgiveness, that you may be feared.
> I wait for the Lord, my soul waits, and in his word I hope;
> my soul waits for the Lord
> more than watchmen for the morning,
> more than watchmen for the morning.
> We hope in the Lord!
> For with the Lord there is steadfast love,
> and with him is plentiful redemption.
> And he will redeem us from all our iniquities
> through Jesus Christ, our Lord. Amen.

—from Psalm 130

God Declares Us Forgiven in Christ
> Scripture Reading: Isaiah 6:6–7

We Thank God
> Hymn: "And Can It Be"

God Speaks to Us from His Word
> Scripture Reading: Isaiah 6
> Sermon

We Dedicate Ourselves to God
> Scripture Reading: Isaiah 6:8
> Hymn: "Take My Life, and Let It Be Consecrated"

God Invites Us to His Throne of Grace
>Scripture Reading: Hebrews 4:16

We Bring Our Supplications to God
>Scripture Reading: Isaiah 6:11a
>Intercessory Prayer

God Sends Us into the World with His Blessing
>Scripture Reading: Isaiah 6:9–13
>Hymn: "Christ for the World We Sing"
>Benediction
>
>>The grace of the Lord Jesus Christ and the love of God and the fellowship of the Holy Spirit be with you all. Amen.

On Campus & Distance Options Available

GRACE BIBLE THEOLOGICAL SEMINARY

Interested in becoming a student or supporting our ministry?
Please visit gbtseminary.org